Managing at the Front Line

Managing at the Front Line

A handbook for managers in social care agencies

Terry Scragg

Managing at the Front Line: A handbook for managers in social care agencies
© Terry Scragg

Terry Scragg has asserted his right in accordance with the *Copyright, Designs and Patents Act 1988* to be identified as the author of this work.

Published by:
Pavilion Publishing (Brighton) Ltd
The Ironworks, Cheapside, Brighton BN1 4GD
Tel: 01273 623222
Fax: 01273 625526
Email: info@pavpub.com
Web: www.pavpub.com

First published 2001

A Catalogue record for this book is available from the British Library.

ISBN 1 84196 064 0

Pavilion is committed to providing high quality, good value training materials and conferences, and bringing new ideas to all those involved in health and social care. Founded by health and social care professionals, Pavilion has maintained its strong links with key agencies in the field, giving us a unique opportunity to help people develop the skills they need through our publications, conferences and training.

Editor: Julia Brennan

Cover design: Luke Jefford

Design and layout: Luke Jefford

Printed by: Ashford Press (Southampton)

Contents

Acknowledgements

I would like to thank Worcestershire Social Services for commissioning this handbook and for agreeing to sponsor its publication. I had considerable guidance and support from many staff in Worcestershire, who assisted in different ways and gave freely of their time, including Gloria Armitage, Tracy Beaver, Liz Clegg, Ann Binney, Patrick Birch, Dennis Buckley, Allan Craig, Gurdev Bhamber, Peter Gilbert, Peter Gillett, Nadine Gregory, Glyn Jones, Tony Leak, Christine Lewington, Sandy Melhuish, Jonathan Monks, Linda Mosely and Celia Willis.

I would also like to thank those students on post-qualifying social work and management programmes at University College Chichester who responded to requests for information, and Giles Darvill of the National Institute for Social Work who was helpful at an early stage of the development of the handbook, suggesting ideas for inclusion and pointing me in the direction of useful publications.

Lastly, my special thanks to Susan who supported and encouraged me throughout the time taken to prepare this handbook.

Terry Scragg
University College Chichester

Foreword

Management can be tough because it brings together the professional and the personal. At the front line in social care particularly, the day-to-day lives of those in contact with services will add their own weight to the task. This handbook is realistic and heartening. It reminds us that all new jobs are difficult. That the cycle of learning moves forward if you are open to your experiences. And that it always gets more rewarding as confidence grows from practice.

As a manager you are responsible for things that matter – the quality of the service offered, the development of your staff, the proper use of the resources made available to you. You may be concerned about the balance between these activities, or how to achieve the compromises necessary to act without letting down your values and standards. The material here will help with the practical solutions to these dilemmas, and link them to how you feel. Only you can achieve that inner harmony which goes with allowing yourself to acknowledge doing well in challenging times. Please let yourself celebrate your successes and those of your team.

You will need to develop your own leadership approaches. Ones that fit your team, your place in the organisation and your preferred ways of working and presenting yourself. As a manager you will be watched and copied, so you need to check with your closest supporters (and even occasionally your potential critics) that you use a range of styles appropriate to the occasion and that you modernise them as you would update your service. It is my personal view that there is no place for rudeness or tantrums in social care management – and that raising your voice more than rarely will be seriously bad for your health. You will have worked these things out for yourself but please be as reflective as you would want your staff to be on their interpersonal behaviour.

I have been a manager in very different organisations, statutory, voluntary and private for a few decades now. I try to remember the achievements when times are difficult, and to find time to learn from the mistakes and how to stop them recurring. We are all different, but it still takes me a lot of personal courage to confront unreasonable behaviour or to deal with people who play power games. This handbook would have given me lots of help had it been around when I first started out. It would not have changed my mind though – taking responsibility as a manager is worth doing and learning to do well.

Jennifer Bernard

About this handbook

This handbook has been written in response to the needs of newly appointed managers in social services departments and other social care services to help them understand more fully some of the key aspects of managing at the front line of services. In response to this demand, Worcestershire Social Services Department kindly agreed to sponsor the handbook and make available facilities to research those aspects of management that would be most useful to staff.

Who is this handbook for?

The handbook is for managers who are working in a range of roles in social services departments and other social care services. What they all have in common is management responsibility for a team (or teams) of people who are providing services directly to users and carers, either in field, day or residential care settings.

Why has it been written?

It has been written to help improve management skills, whether for a newly appointed frontline manager, or for managers who have been managing for some time, but feel they could benefit from reflecting on aspects of their management practice.

The approach taken in this handbook is informed by discussion with frontline managers in Worcestershire Social Services Department and post-qualifying social work and management students attending courses at University College Chichester. Additional ideas came from training courses I have led over many years in a wide range of public sector organisations.

How will this handbook help me?

The handbook is organised in a way that makes it easy for you to look up specific aspects of management and is intended to help you improve your management skills or plan how you will manage a particular function in the future.

The handbook offers you:

- an overview of the responsibilities of the frontline manager

- an opportunity to reflect on your performance as a frontline manager in relation to the areas featured in the handbook

- reference to theoretical models of management to enable you to relate your approach to management to research findings

- examples from managers and practitioners that may help you place your own experience in a wider context

- a resource which should prove helpful to you as you engage in management development activities.

How can I best use this handbook?

How you decide to use this handbook will very much depend on your needs. It is first and foremost a practical resource to support you and is not intended to be read from cover to cover. It focuses on a number of key areas which have been highlighted by staff who were interviewed or participated in a survey which asked for suggested areas for inclusion. It is intended to be a source of ideas, information and examples of management practice which can be consulted when you are looking to improve your own performance in the management role.

It should be stressed that a handbook of this nature cannot possibly cover all aspects of managing at the front line and some important areas of practice have been dealt with superficially. Should you want to explore a particular issue in more depth, then turn to the **Appendix 1** which lists suggestions for texts, journals and websites where you can access further information on the topics covered in the handbook.

Managing at the front line:
Changing roles and responsibilities

Introduction

It is gratifying to witness an increasingly wide range of statements from the Government and researchers which highlight the pivotal role played by frontline managers in social services departments and other social care services. Two recent statements sum up the growing awareness of the importance of the frontline manager's role:

> *'Frontline managers are the keystones of any social services organisation. Their quality and competence makes a significant difference to its performance.'*
>
> (Social Services Inspectorate, 1999)

> *'Better management is a central requirement if long-term care is to meet the modern requirements of its residents, their relatives, regulators and purchasers.'*
>
> (Johnson* et al*, 1999)

What is frontline management?

Although the role of the frontline manager may vary according to the requirements of the employing organisation and particular responsibilities of a post, there are common features in all frontline management posts. All frontline managers have the authority and responsibility for planning and controlling the work of a group of staff through close contact.

They are responsible for implementing policies at the point where it impacts on people using the service, and are typically team leaders and managers of a residential, day or domiciliary service. In this sense they are the visible managers of the organisation, and often the public face of management in the organisation.

Due to their influence in supporting and supervising staff and ensuring the development of high quality practice, the frontline manager and his/her responsibilities play a crucial role in the success of the organisation and consequently the quality of services provided. It has been claimed that frontline managers can make or break top management plans due to their crucial role in the implementation of organisational strategies, which gives some sense of the importance of the role as stated by the Chief Inspector of Social Services (see **page 3**).

The changing role of the frontline manager

Impact of Government policy on frontline managers

As social services departments and other social care agencies respond to an increasing range of Government initiatives, particularly the emphasis on improving standards of performance across all areas of service delivery, the responsibility for implementing these initiatives falls directly on frontline managers and their staff. Frontline managers therefore have an important leadership role at the point of service delivery, where they are central to the process of translating policy into practice.

How has the role changed?

The role of the frontline manager has changed significantly, particularly over the last ten years, along with the wider changes that have taken place in local government and other public sector organisations. This has resulted from the move towards flatter management structures and greater devolved responsibility to the front line of services, linked to the need to develop more localised and responsive services.

Motivating and supporting staff

These changes mean that frontline managers have a critical role in aligning the strategies and objectives of the organisation with the work of practitioners and other staff. The growing emphasis on performance management means that frontline managers need to lead and motivate staff to achieve the high standards of practice which are a requirement of all services. It also means managers require a much greater understanding of staff's core competencies in order to meet the demands on the service, as well as a sensitivity to staff's needs as they work under increasing pressure.

Key tasks emerging from this changed role

Although it is possible to list a wide range of activities that are now considered the responsibility of frontline managers, there is a core of activities which managers interviewed for this publication have identified as a priority.

The frontline manager:
Your place in your organisation

Clarity about the goals of the service

As a frontline manager you need to be clear about the mission or purpose of your service. It is from the mission statement that the strategies and policies are developed, and the activities of practitioners are designed to contribute to the achievement of organisational strategies. This has become more important with the greater devolvement of responsibility to the front line and the need to relate departmental strategies to the activities of practitioners. This is about communicating the 'bigger picture' to team members so that they understand what the organisation is trying to achieve and how their contribution as practitioners fits in with this bigger picture. Securing agreement on how individuals and teams will work to achieve departmental goals is an essential part of the frontline manager's responsibility. Without this agreement it is less likely that staff will feel their contribution is valued, and consequently will feel less motivated to work to achieve departmental goals.

Knowledge of the task

Frontline managers are usually recruited from the ranks of practitioners, and as such bring to the role a detailed understanding of practice. They also bring the skills to deal promptly at first hand with problems arising at the point of service delivery, in order to direct, guide and advise practitioners as appropriate. It is the detailed understanding of the work of practitioners that is important in enabling frontline managers to make appropriate decisions and respond to staff as they struggle with the daily demands and contradictions of practice.

Being available to staff

Frontline managers operate in the 'here and now' for much of their time. This means being available for immediate advice and consultation on a day-to-day basis, identifying problems, responding rapidly to the concerns of staff and initiating or supporting corrective action as required. The complexity of the work means that frequent recourse to the manager will always be needed by some staff.

Supporting staff through supervision and consultation

With staff under increasing pressure as services become ever more responsive and concentrate their scarce resources on the most needy, it is recognised in many social services departments that staff supervision and consultation play a crucial role in supporting and maintaining staff morale. Similarly, a knowledge of practice is also important when providing supervision – the practitioner's reflection of their work with service users benefits from the manager's understanding of the complexity of practice situations.

Maintaining quality standards

Frontline managers play an important role in influencing and developing standards of practice in their teams. They have both a quality control function (monitoring the provision of services provided) and a quality assurance function (ensuring services are provided to a particular standard and meet service users' needs), and have the responsibility for taking corrective action when necessary.

Managing performance

Closely related to the maintenance of quality standards is the increased emphasis on managing performance which is primarily concerned with relating key organisational objectives to the activities of the individuals and teams. Frontline managers are required to understand the quality standards for their service, both qualitative and quantitative, and to measure the performance of the service being provided against these standards. This can mean taking action when performance falls below acceptable levels and the work of individual members of staff is unsatisfactory.

Developing a commitment to work-based learning

Lastly, but by no means less important is the frontline manager's crucial role in work-based learning, both for themselves and their staff. Formal education and training play an important role in developing professional expertise, but most learning is work-based, arising naturally out of the demands and challenges of the work itself (for example, solving problems, improving quality or coping with change through interactions in the workplace with colleagues and users of services). The quality of management is highly significant, particularly the potential for creating a climate that facilitates work-based learning, and contributes to the development of the service.

The link between the top of the organisation and the front line

Frontline managers are located at a point in organisations which is critical for the effectiveness of the service. They are the channel for the transmission of information from senior management to the front line, and in turn they transmit information upwards through the organisation so that senior managers have a clear sense of what is happening at the front line.

In playing this role the frontline manager is the 'hinge' between senior management and the needs of frontline staff, interpreting the goals of the department to practitioners. It is critical to the success of an organisation to communicate and explain management decisions, and this in turn provides information where policies are not working and also represents the opinions of frontline staff to senior managers.

Working with individuals and teams

Social workers, social care staff and support staff are an organisation's main asset, and the deployment of this important resource is a key responsibility of frontline managers. Management is primarily about getting things done through others in a way which is consistent with the organisation's strategy. This means that managers are responsible for co-ordinating work activities based on service priorities, guiding and supporting staff and monitoring performance. To achieve these objectives, management is primarily a social activity where sensitivity and understanding of other members of the team is essential in order to match the knowledge and skills with the service requirements.

Holding together the different worlds of social services

Frontline managers are in a key position to hold together what can seem like different worlds, integrating the work of practitioners with the wider activities of the organisation and avoiding the split that can develop when frontline managers fail to achieve the integration between the work of practitioners and the demands of the wider department, and ultimately, Government. The increasing demands on frontline managers mean that their traditional orientation towards practice has been partly diverted by concern for the management of resources. If this tension is not understood and discussed in the team it can lead to a split in identity and loyalties. It is the bridge between the front line and management which avoids the danger of staff identifying completely with either practice or management and neglecting to relate wider organisational needs to the realities of practice.

The link between the team, other parts of the organisation and the wider community

Frontline managers play an increasingly important role at the boundaries of their team or unit and other parts of the organisation – for example between senior management and direct practice staff, the team and other teams within the organisation, and at the boundaries with other services. Both internally and externally, these relationships are of growing importance as local authorities work more corporately and manage the growing partnership arrangements with other services.

KEY POINTS

○ It is now recognised that frontline managers play a crucial role in developing and enhancing the performance of social care services.

○ The demands on frontline managers have increased as a result of flatter management structures and more devolved responsibilities to the front line.

○ Frontline managers need to relate the goals for their service to the activities of staff at the front line in order to meet wider organisational strategies.

○ Frontline managers have a number of key responsibilities, including being available to staff, providing supervision and consultation and supporting work-based learning to achieve high quality services.

○ Frontline managers play an important role in linking with different parts of the organisation and those services that influence work at the front line.

Introduction

All staff experience, to varying degrees, a period of transition when they are first appointed to a management post. Research by John Lawler and Jeff Hearn (1997) found that staff appointed to their first management post often had considerable doubts about their confidence to carry out the required tasks. Managers reported not having sufficient preparation or training for the management role. This research confirms the accounts of managers I have worked with who often felt unprepared for the management role and endured an uncomfortable period as they adjusted to the demands of a new job.

As John Harris and Des Kelly (1992) observe, you may have been pushed or pulled towards the new job for a variety of reasons, but getting the job was a high spot which can be quickly followed by a sense of anti-climax as the demands and the difficulties associated with the new post move into the foreground. We should of course remember that these feelings are common when someone moves into a new job or role.

Traditionally, appointments to management posts in social services departments and social care agencies are social workers and others in similar direct care roles whose formal training and development have been directed to creating an effective practitioner. I will assume you have derived (to varying degrees) satisfaction from performing effectively in the practitioner role, that you are likely to have been promoted to a management post on the assumption of your competence as a practitioner, and that you have demonstrated the potential to manage the service.

New demands

With the move into management you are now required to develop an additional range of knowledge and skills specifically concerned with management. Although writers on social work and social care stress the work of the practitioner as a solid grounding for management (for example, making decisions, influencing outcomes, seeking solutions to novel problems) moving into management means personal change in a number of ways:

- you may have been promoted from within the same team and now assume responsibility for the work of people who were previously your colleagues

- your relationship with practitioners and colleagues changes when you take on a management role

- you have to adapt to expectations of practitioners and others so that you can act decisively in a wide range of situations

- you have to learn the language and norms of management and how to work effectively in a new department or, if you are in the same department, where there will be different expectations placed on you.

Practitioner or manager?

Of course being promoted to a management role doesn't mean that you have to jettison your specialist role. You may continue to play a dual role both as a specialist and a manager. Depending on the arrangement in your particular situation, you may need to undertake specialist activities from time to time (several team leaders spoke of the need to occasionally cover for colleagues, or of times when their greater experience or skill was needed in a particular situation). Although there are often tensions in managing these dual roles, you should as far as possible develop strategies with your team to enable you to develop the managerial aspects of your role.

Some managers interviewed suggested that although they were keen to develop their managerial role they missed some aspects of their former specialist role and took opportunities to be both practitioners and managers. These included:

- 'keeping their hand in' as a specialist practitioner
- demonstrating to staff that they could still perform in the specialist role
- feeling comfortable carrying out tasks where they had developed high levels of skill in their previous role
- being seen to 'get stuck in' alongside colleagues when resources were limited.

Although you may need to undertake some practitioner tasks, the main emphasis should be on the development of your management role. Vivien Martin (2000) has suggested several ways of developing this role, for example:

- guiding or coaching staff to improve their specialist skills, thereby helping members of your team develop new competencies
- developing the competencies of staff, rather than feeling you should take over tasks that are within their capabilities
- demonstrating leadership skills through involving team members in discussions about objectives, planning and organising tasks and looking at how they could monitor and evaluate outcomes
- taking action to secure additional resources or to manage levels of activity so they are within your team's resource capabilities. (You may, of course, need to respond to crises or emergencies, but these should not become frequent)
- demonstrating your effectiveness as a manager to your line manager and department through your performance in the management role, particularly in terms of the motivation and morale in your team.

Where you are required to maintain both specialist practitioner and management roles you could usefully reflect on the boundaries between the roles and develop awareness of what you should focus on to be effective in the management role.

Managerial and practitioner roles – the 'hybrid manager'

Many staff I have worked with are appointed to a management role but still have a professional or practitioner role and have to balance the demands of the two competing elements of their work. When you are in this position it is important to clarify the two roles and ascertain which elements are separate and which overlap.

For example, in the diagram below, based on an example of a residential manager working in a children's service, there is considerable overlap in the roles.

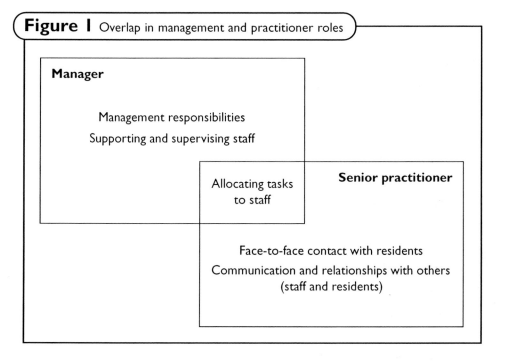

Figure 1 Overlap in management and practitioner roles

Manager

Management responsibilities
Supporting and supervising staff

Allocating tasks
to staff

Senior practitioner

Face-to-face contact with residents
Communication and relationships with others
(staff and residents)

This is similar to Veronica Coulshed's (1990) statement that all social workers are managers. Whether the people managed are staff or service users, there are many opportunities for the transfer of knowledge. However, if you maintain both a specialist and a management role you need to be clear about the respective responsibilities of each role and the boundaries between them.

ACTIVITY

Compare the example on page 13 with your own role and activities. How can you achieve an appropriate balance between the two roles? Write down your ideas on a sheet of paper.

The process of transition

The period of transition means that as a newly appointed manager you have to learn what is required of you to perform effectively in the new role and adapt to the demands of the organisation. It is common for managers to describe their initial period in the new role as one where their confidence dropped for a period as the difficulties associated with the new role become more apparent.

'After I was promoted I felt de-skilled initially. My confidence dropped and I didn't feel I could contribute to management meetings.'

Team manager

Stages of transition

The transition to the management role means you are undergoing a change. Although you may feel particularly good about yourself before the transition, the challenge of the new job can lead to feelings that are common to many forms of transition, including personal crisis or enforced changes. There are a number of stages that are typically involved in any transition. For example, Andrew Kakabadse and colleagues (1988) have described a series of phases in the transition to a new role in terms of three phases, as described below.

Phase 1: Getting used to new responsibilities

Whether or not you have changed organisations, your job content is different. As you become familiar with your new responsibilities and new environment your effectiveness is likely to drop. Once you become used to the new environment and processes – hopefully with the help and guidance of colleagues – you will begin to feel your old sense of self emerging. The reactions you may experience at this stage include immobilisation and denial.

Immobilisation

Feelings of threat and being overwhelmed. Your level of knowledge and understanding may not be able to meet expectations, and the way that things are done in the organisation is unfamiliar. You may feel that you can make very little contribution at this stage.

Denial

With feelings of immobilisation it is likely that you may find yourself holding on to your previous ways of working. You may idealise your former role as a way of managing the change needed in your new role. Some managers may wish they could return to their former role.

Phase 2: Re-learning

When you have begun to become familiar with the new environment and some of the work processes, you have to start learning about the new responsibilities and job skills that accompany the role of manager. You will also have to develop or adapt your relationship with other managers and colleagues and begin to understand their way of doing things and the expected norms of behaviour. This requires a rapid learning curve and can be accompanied by feelings of depression as you realise that you can no longer apply many of your old skills.

Depression

Depression can affect you if the new demands on you are ones that you don't feel you can meet. You may have felt that you had developed your knowledge and skills in the practitioner role to a high degree, and you are now faced with situations where you don't feel competent. This stage of the transition can lead to feelings of panic and helplessness, although it is the first step in re-learning as you realise your level of performance has dropped and you need to let go of the past.

Acceptance

Moving on from feelings of depression can be the turning point in the transition when you feel comfortable to acknowledge the new challenges of the role and begin to leave behind your former role. You are letting go of the past and accepting the new reality. You are beginning to see yourself more positively and there is a growing satisfaction with the new role.

Phase 3: Becoming effective

Becoming effective in the frontline role means successfully negotiating the transition. You have let go of your past role, have accepted the new reality and challenges, and so become more proactive. You can now start to experiment with new behaviours, new ways of working and new approaches. This final stage of the transition is where new behaviours and attitudes are incorporated into what is left of the old role and ways of working. You have now consolidated your position and feel more confident than when you first moved into the management role.

Letting go of the old role

A significant step to moving smoothly through this period of transition is to let go of the previous role. Managers can find themselves still undertaking tasks associated with their previous job role, and sometimes carrying out aspects of the job – particularly if they have been promoted within the same department or team. To establish yourself effectively it is necessary to let go of the old role before you can begin the transition to the new one. There can be a number of reasons for unwillingness to let go, including reluctance to leave the safety of the old role and concern about the risks or uncertainty of the new role, particularly where there are unclear expectations or definitions.

Internalisation

This is the final stage of the transition where you find behaviours and attitudes are incorporated into what remains of your former attitudes and behaviour. You are now consolidating your position and operating at a higher level than when you were first appointed and are beginning to gain satisfaction from the management role.

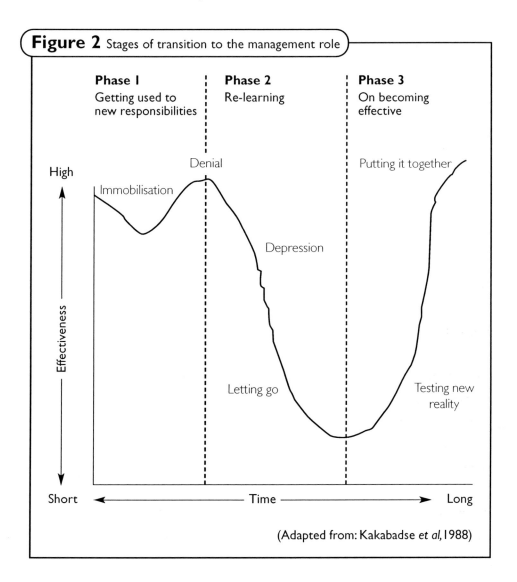

Figure 2 Stages of transition to the management role

Phase 1
Getting used to
new responsibilities

Phase 2
Re-learning

Phase 3
On becoming
effective

High

Denial

Putting it together

Immobilisation

Effectiveness

Depression

Letting go

Testing new
reality

Short ← Time → Long

(Adapted from: Kakabadse et al, 1988)

Changed relationship with staff

As Barbara Hearn and colleagues (1992) point out, as a manager you are now in a hierarchical position in relation to staff, and that must be acknowledged. Accepting this change is an important part of the transition and one that managers describe as often difficult to adjust to, particularly as they see themselves as team colleague but also as manager. This is often further complicated by promotion within the same team.

A number of managers interviewed confirmed the view that it is necessary to accept a managerial identity and the responsibilities that go with that identity. This is a key change in the transition from practitioner to manager and can prove to be an identity crisis for some managers.

'The crunch came one day soon after I became a team leader. I knew I had to rethink my role and my relationship with the team. It was part of becoming a manager. I couldn't be everybody's buddy anymore. I'm responsible for their work now and I've had to think myself into the new job and acknowledge the responsibility that went with it.'

Team manager

Managing the transition

Who can help?

In the past it was common for managers to be 'thrown in at the deep end' without proper induction, briefing and support, as reported by several managers interviewed.

It is important to identify both formal and informal support within the organisation. Other managers who will have experienced a similar transition will be able to empathise with you and suggest ways of coping. Your own line manager has a major responsibility here to support you and identify development opportunities that can improve your skills (although some managers did not feel confident to be open about their support needs with their line managers).

When you are developing your management skills it is important to share your feelings in an open and frank way so that you enable others to support you. Discussion with other managers can help you make sense of the process of transition. There are risks for managers in that they can become isolated when they feel under pressure to appear competent both with staff and other management colleagues. This is not healthy for the individual or the organisation and is one of the less attractive consequences of the 'macho management' culture in found in some public sector organisations.

Organisations which understand the relationship between individual and organisation effectiveness provide a more structured approach, including induction and enhanced support, particularly from a line manager. Other approaches include the appointment of a mentor who meets periodically with the newly appointed manager to review progress and is available for consultation during the period of transition.

Different reactions to the transition

It is important to stress that not everyone who moves into a management role will have the same reactions as those described in the process of transition. How quickly you adjust to the new post will be dependent on a range of factors, including your feelings about the change of role, an awareness of the demands of the management role, the support and guidance provided by the organisation through induction and support from a line manager and the rapport established with team members.

'It's important to establish what your responsibilities are and clarity about your boundaries and lines of responsibility and the expectations of your manager and your staff. You can't begin to work effectively until your are clear what your "fit" is with your boss and the team.'

Team manager

(KEY POINTS)

○ It is still common for managers to be appointed with little preparation for the new role and consequently to feel unprepared for the role.

○ It is often assumed, erroneously, that competence in a practitioner role is the basis for management ability, rather than acknowledging that management requires the development of new knowledge and skills.

○ Following the excitement and anticipation of the new role, the transition to management is often uncomfortable and you may feel de-skilled for a period, with feelings of ineffectiveness. This is a normal reaction.

○ It is necessary to let go of the old role before adopting the new one, acknowledging the value of practitioner skills but recognising the importance of learning how to become effective as a manager.

○ It takes time to learn about a new organisation and new role.

○ The length of the transition will depend on your ability to adjust to the demands of the new role. Time and a positive engagement with the new role and its demands will quickly lead to feeling effective as you gain new knowledge and skills.

○ Requesting an induction and briefing on the new role, and identifying and asking for support (whether formally or informally) is important and can be a great help during the transition to the new role.

○ Your experience of the transition to the management role is important as it can help you understand how staff may feel on appointment to a new post or when they take on new responsibilities. This can provide pointers to how you may be able to support staff as they experience the process of transition.

The work of the manager

Introduction

The task of the frontline manager is becoming much clearer as a result of evidence from services, particularly the development of occupational standards, core competencies and the outcomes of reviews of departments. These developments are helping overcome one of the traditional problems of newly appointed managers – having to make choices between competing demands but never quite knowing whether their efforts are appropriate. This is particularly so if they have not received detailed briefing on the key objectives for their service, or have received little feedback on their performance from their line manager.

One useful activity when you are newly appointed is to spend some time examining some of the better known research on what managers do, the roles they play and how they develop their priorities (see **Appendix 1**). You can then use this information to reflect on your own approach to management and whether you feel your activities are appropriate to your role and tasks, and whether you are achieving the objectives for your service as a result of these activities.

What managers actually do

Colin Hales (1993) compared eight studies of management work and found a number of similar elements in all the studies. The common activities included the manager:

- as the figurehead or leader of a work unit, representing it and acting as its point of contact
- monitoring and disseminating information

- negotiating with staff, other managers and people and services outside the organisation at different levels
- monitoring the flow of work, solving problems and dealing with disruptions
- allocating resources
- directing and controlling the work of staff
- developing contacts and liaising with others
- planning what is to be done, and when
- innovating and seeking ways to improve the work of the team.

The reality of management practice

Although the traditional account of management is one of carrying out functions such as planning, organising, motivating, controlling and co-ordinating, the reality can be very different. From this research, Hales went on to describe the usual day-to-day activities of a manager, suggesting that they spend most of their time in a typically fragmented day, switching attention frequently from one person to another and from one subject to another, reacting to events and requests from staff and others and continually negotiating over resources. Much of this activity takes place with people and involves a high level of face-to-face communication.

You will note from these findings that managers are concerned with responding to people and events around them. This paints a picture of the manager continually driven to a large extent by those day-to-day issues which require a response. This is an understandable situation where frontline managers are in close contact with their staff and faced with situations requiring urgent consultation and decision-making on a daily basis.

ACTIVITY

1. How far does Hales's description of management tasks and the way managers work compare with your own way of working?

....

....

....

....

2. What does this say about your management?

....

....

....

....

3. What does it suggest about how you use your time?

....

....

....

....

4. Are you getting the priorities correct or do you need to develop alternative ways of working to achieve greater effectiveness?

....

....

....

....

Continued…

ACTIVITY continued

5. How much are your activities contributing to the key objectives for your team?

....

....

....

....

Taking control of your activities

In order to develop your effectiveness in the frontline management role you need to take control of your activities, particularly your time, in order to work towards the achievement of the objectives for your service. This requires you to think about which activities will contribute most to the achievement of the objectives, and managing the time pressures which result in you dealing with situations in a superficial manner. The next piece of research examines the roles managers play and should help you to identify the skills needed to develop your effectiveness in the frontline role.

Managerial roles

The second major research study was carried out by Henry Mintzberg (1990), who examined the work of five senior managers in an attempt to classify the essential functions of management at this level in an organisation. Although these findings relate to a small number of senior managers, the findings have been usefully applied to managers at all levels in a range of organisations. He found that managers have a set of 10 different roles which he grouped under three broad headings: interpersonal, informational and decisional.

Interpersonal roles

These three roles are all concerned with the manager's relationship with other people based on the manager's status and authority:

- the **figurehead role** with the manager as symbol and representative of the organisation
- the **leadership role** where the manager has the authority and responsibility for staffing and the motivation and guidance of staff
- the **liaison role** which involves the manager in relationships with staff within the organisation as well as external relationships with other organisations as part of their work in linking the organisation to the wider environment.

Informational roles

These roles are concerned with communicating information internally and externally.

- The **monitor role** involves the manager receiving information both from internal and external sources and transmitting it to others.
- The **disseminator role** involves the manager, working according to the liaison role, transmitting information to external organisations as well as internally between the manager and staff.
- The **spokesperson role** is concerned with giving information to the general public and to people of influence.

Decisional roles

Under this heading Mintzberg placed four roles which are concerned with the strategic direction of the organisation.

- The **entrepreneurial role** is concerned with the manager's function to initiate change and plan for its implementation.
- The **disturbance handler role** involves the manager responding to events outside their control and to unpredictable situations, and making decisions to counter these occurrences.
- The **resource allocator role** involves the manager in making choices about the allocation of money, staff, time and equipment.
- The **negotiator role** sees the manager participating along with others in making decisions about the commitment of resources.

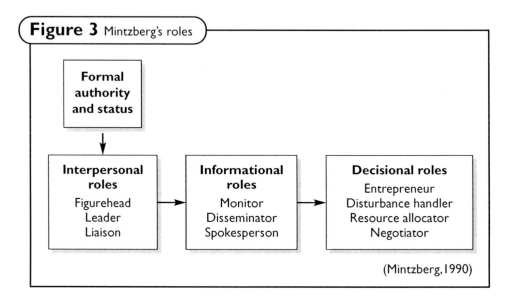

Figure 3 Mintzberg's roles

Formal authority and status

Interpersonal roles	Informational roles	Decisional roles
Figurehead	Monitor	Entrepreneur
Leader	Disseminator	Disturbance handler
Liaison	Spokesperson	Resource allocator
		Negotiator

(Mintzberg, 1990)

ACTIVITY

Mintzberg's roles

Reflect on your recent pattern of work and try to identify where you have undertaken activities that relate to one or more of Mintzberg's roles.

- **Interpersonal roles:** for example when you represented your team internally in your organisation and externally with other organisations.

- **Informational roles:** for example where you sought information on behalf of your team and transmitted it to team members.

- **Decisional roles:** for example where you have made decisions about the allocation of scarce resources in order to improve service delivery.

Although Mintzberg's research focused on senior managers, you will probably have found that you have played some or all of these roles recently. Mintzberg does caution, however, that management is more an art than a science, and managers choose to emphasise different roles depending on the situation they are managing. As a result, the degree to which these roles is carried out is likely to vary from one manager and one situation to another. You will probably emphasise some of these roles more than others depending on your own particular interests and the particular requirements of the service.

What Mintzberg's findings do suggest is that you need to use your interpersonal skills in order to obtain and interpret information, and that this information should then be used to make decisions.

Demands, constraints and choices – the differences in what managers do

The final piece of research which is helpful in exploring what managers do, and which links with the idea of managers emphasising different aspects of their role, is the work of Rosemary Stewart (1997). Stewart found that managers in similar jobs differ in what they do, with each manager doing the job in their own way. She believes this is because managers see their job differently, and that individual managers focus on particular aspects and ignore others. Managers also have different skills, and this leads them to give more time to the things they are good at or interested in, and this influences how they spend their time.

Stewart has described this as the **demands, constraints** and **choices** that all managers have in relation to their role.

Demands: these are the 'must dos'– the levels of accountability that must be achieved – and usually refer to meeting your organisation's expectations. In particular, they refer to meeting the expectations of your line manager and staff about what should be done. Further demands can arise from the expectations of people outside the organisation, for example staff in other services with whom you are working in partnership.

Constraints: these are the factors, both internally and externally, that limit what you can do. These can include: resources, legal requirements, policies and procedures and others' attitudes and expectations.

Choices: these are the opportunities you have to decide what you want to do and how you do it. This is the area where you can emphasise some aspects of your job and give lower priority to or ignore others. As a frontline manager you are likely to find your scope for choice is somewhat restricted, but you will still have scope for making choices about which aspects of the role you will develop.

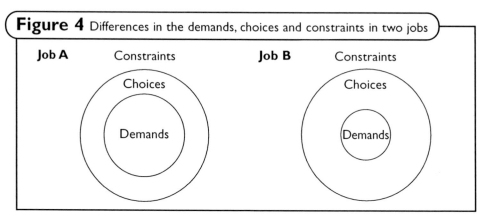

Figure 4 Differences in the demands, choices and constraints in two jobs

You have more choices than you think

Commenting on Stewart's research, Ian Cunningham (1994) suggests that the less successful manager is likely to see themselves as having less choice than the outside observer might identify. Such managers can make false assumptions about the demands and constraints in their situation but fail to test them. The more successful manager tends to see more choices, which Cunningham sees as linked to feelings of autonomy and willingness to push the boundaries of the job. The successful manager is likely to have a good 'map' of the 'territory' in which they operate and work in a culture which encourages them to break out of any self-imposed straightjacket.

ACTIVITY

1. What are some of the demands your job makes on you?
   For example: internally imposed, externally imposed or self-imposed.

   ....

   ....

   ....

   ....

Continued…

ACTIVITY continued

2. What are the constraints on you?
   For example: resources, legal, work processes, policies and procedures, other people's attitudes and expectations, your own attitudes and beliefs.

   ....

   ....

   ....

   ....

3. What choices do you have?
   For example: what work you wish to do, how you wish to accomplish it, when you do it, what areas of the service you would like to develop.

   ....

   ....

   ....

   ....

Once you have completed this activity you should have a clearer understanding of the demands, constraints and choices in your frontline manager role. It will have helped you identify the demands and the constraints of your job and what opportunities exist in the space between demands and constraints for you to decide what you want to do and how you will do it. In other words, you are shaping the job around your preferred activities, roles and styles of working.

KEY POINTS

○ What other managers actually do, as understood from research findings, can be helpful in identifying the main activities common to managers.

○ Managers, by the nature of their work and particularly in frontline roles, tend to work in ways that emphasise responsiveness and are concerned with the here and now and problem-solving.

○ Managerial roles can help you identify those activities that you can develop in order to provide a clearer focus on the future.

○ All managers are faced with demands and constraints but also have choices. Identifying the gap between demands and constraints can offer the opportunity to shape the job in the way you want.

Developing your effectiveness
as a frontline manager

Introduction

Managing in a social services department inevitably means responding
to multiple demands and expectations in terms of the many goals you
must achieve. Becoming more effective in your frontline role can be
achieved if you are clear about what is expected of you and therefore set
yourself priorities, if you are able to manage your time and consequently
have more time to attend to the priority tasks, and if you are able to
delegate tasks which team members can carry out more appropriately.

Organisational strategies and objectives

Being clear about what is expected of you in your role stems from an
understanding of the corporate strategies for the service and the strategic
objectives and how these relate to your team objectives. This will enable
you to interpret them, communicate them to team members and implement
them more effectively with the support of the team. Understanding strategy
will also help you in deciding what tasks are a priority, what you should be
achieving in wider organisational terms, and what you will be judged against
in performance terms as a frontline manager.

Strategic objectives

These are usually few in number and stated in broad terms. They should
be (ideally) communicated by senior managers to frontline managers who
are then required to translate them into specific objectives which determine
the focus and content of the work of the team on a day-to-day basis.

ACTIVITY

1. What are the strategies of your organisation?

....

....

....

2. What are the key objectives?

....

....

....

3. What are the implications of these objectives for your team?

....

....

....

4. Are you able to translate corporate level strategies and objectives into individual objectives for staff?

....

....

....

Team and individual objectives

Determining team and individual objectives is a process that involves working with your line manager to interpret how the department's strategic objectives can be met through the work of your team as well as discussion with your team about these objectives and how they can be achieved by the work of individual members of staff.

In order to do this effectively you need to work with your team and establish the specific operational objectives and how the team's efforts fit into the overall organisational strategic objectives. This activity enables staff to feel they are contributing to the achievement of the organisational strategies and that their practice is important to the organisation's success.

Once these have been agreed, and ideally this should be with your line manager, they need to be discussed with staff. In your discussion you should focus on the ways in which the objectives for the team can be translated into individual objectives, to enable team members to participate in discussing the best way of achieving them. This is also an opportunity for feedback on the scope for implementation and the chances of success in implementing strategy.

The quality of objectives

A measure of your effectiveness as a manager is the development of objectives which help team members focus on the essentials in terms of their practice. A small number of critical objectives should be identified which are seen as practical by staff and important to the service. Reaching agreement with your team members on a small number of objectives should be your aim. Remember, it is demotivating to set objectives that are unrealistic and unachievable and are not seen as important by staff.

ACTIVITY

Check that your objectives:

- are **realistic** – achievable within the resources available
- are as **specific as possible** so that it is clear when they have been achieved
- are **agreed with the staff** who will carry them out or be affected by their implementation
- can be **reviewed** and adjusted as necessary
- have a **target date** for achievement.

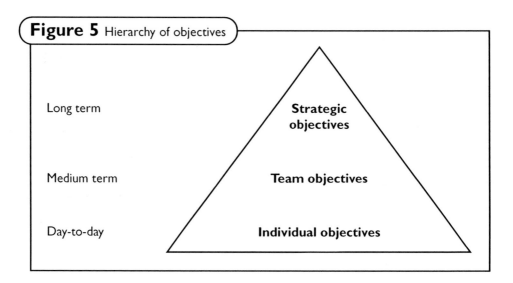

Figure 5 Hierarchy of objectives

Long term — Strategic objectives

Medium term — Team objectives

Day-to-day — Individual objectives

'Worcestershire Social Services hold regular meetings for frontline managers where they are briefed on policy and strategy. These are led by senior managers who see them as crucial in working through current and future challenges and communicating key messages to the frontline managers. It is expected that frontline managers will in turn communicate department policy to staff teams in order that there is a clear connection between the strategic direction of the service and individual practice.'

Senior manager

Establishing priorities

Once you are clear about the objectives for your team you can begin to make priorities about how you will meet them. You need to make choices about priorities, recognising that there are often conflicting demands. Based on ideas from John Harris and Des Kelly (1992), three potential areas of conflict are:

● **between priorities**, for example training staff for new responsibilities at a time when there is pressure to maintain the current output

● **within priorities**, for example having to achieve tasks within specific time limits while recognising that a higher quality outcome requires a longer timescale

- **between short and long-term priorities**, for example making immediate but limited improvements to a service while recognising that long-term improvements are necessary.

When you are deciding priorities you need to keep these competing demands in balance.

Timescales for priorities

Harris and Kelly also caution managers about timescales for priorities. Decisions in which the priority is an immediate operational activity need little lead time; decisions in which the priority is budgetary require a longer lead time; decisions concerning changes to staff attitudes, abilities and working relationships take the longest lead time of all.

ACTIVITY

Can you differentiate between your long-term and short-term objectives?

1. Give examples of your long-term objectives.

....

....

....

2. Give examples of your short-term objectives.

....

....

....

3. What are some of the potential conflicts between priorities?

....

....

....

Once you are clear about the objectives for the team and how these will be achieved you are in a stronger position to monitor the progress successfully and to decide what needs to be done to correct any problems that occur in the implementation stage.

Role clarification

A further useful area when trying to improve your effectiveness is to clarify your ideas about what is expected of you and how others feel you should respond in terms of your role. As a frontline manager a wide range of people will have expectations about how you should be behaving. Alan Barlow (1990) has identified three helpful definitions related to role:

- **role relationships:** what you expect of a person because of the job they do. These expectations do not change when the job holder changes role unless the job is redesigned

- **role behaviours:** what your expect of another person because of who they are, rather than the role they perform. These expectations will change with the job holder

- **process expectations:** how the person performs a task.

It is useful to clarify a number of issues when you are making sense of expectations, for example:

- tasks that are not being performed because you do not realise they are part of your role

- tasks that are duplicated because you and someone else see the activities as part of their role

- strained relationships because expectations have not been made clear.

ACTIVITY

Part one

A role map of your job

1. Identify your key work relationships and write down your expectations of them on a blank sheet of paper.

2. For each, write down what you think they think they require from you.

3. On another blank sheet of paper, draw a network of your role relationships, putting names and job titles in the diagram.

4. Emphasise the importance (or otherwise) of the role relationship by the distance at which you place the person from your role. For example, if the importance of the role relationship is low, draw the person further away from your role than if the importance of the role relationship is high.

5. Using this map, pick out the key posts that are crucial to your working effectively.

6. For those people you have chosen, list their expectations of you.

Arrange to meet the people you have listed on your role map and share your views with them, discussing the expectations that each of you hold of each other's roles. In addition:

- identify any areas of conflict and explore the reasons for these

- plan together how you will act to overcome conflicts.

Part two

Action plan

1. The areas that are causing most difficulty are:

. . . .

. . . .

. . . .

2. Our plan of action to deal with these is:

. . . .

. . . .

. . . .

Continued…

ACTIVITY continued

3. We will review progress on:

....

....

....

4. Areas of training and development this exercise has highlighted are:

....

....

....

Managing your time

As a frontline manager you will find yourself having to respond to an endless stream of activities that need your attention. The time you have available to meet these commitments is a fixed resource, it is totally inelastic, and if you are to free up more time it will have to be made through the efficient management of this finite resource. Time management is essentially about priorities. It is recognising what needs to be done and making *that* a priority while at the same time saying 'no' to some activities and delegating work to others where appropriate. In addition, it is important to check that what you are doing reflects your priorities from time to time.

Putting time into a wider context

Time management is a popular topic in management training courses, as it is an important area of managerial effectiveness. However, you should not view your use of time in isolation from other aspects of your management, such as leadership, (see **Chapter 5**) delegation and your wish to be visible and available to staff, both for consultation and supervision. How you see yourself as a manager and the style of management you want to create will have implications for your use of time and for the decisions you will need to make about what you see as priority tasks.

ACTIVITY

In the context of frontline management it is useful to think about how you are currently using your time.

Think about the following questions, jotting down your ideas on a sheet of paper.

1. Do you know what the main tasks are? Answering this question should give you ideas about what you should be spending time on to be more effective.

2. Do you know what you are currently spending your time on – are these the right activities?

3. Do you reflect on the difference between what you should be doing and what you are doing? Does this tell you what needs changing?

4. Now decide how you will change your use of time.

5. Review your progress periodically to ensure that your approach is working.

Once you have worked through this activity you should be in a position to think of some activities which could improve your use of time. For example:

- delegating work to others
- planning and scheduling your time carefully, thinking about the main demands on your time
- using your diary, planning ahead, working back from deadlines for the completion of reports etc
- making a list of your key activities each day and reviewing it at the end of the day
- keeping information you need regularly (eg telephone numbers) close to hand
- allowing yourself time to 'walk the job'
- creating a filing system which works and which allows for information to be retrieved quickly.

In the end, managing your time involves thinking about your job and its main demands, analysing how you use your time and setting priorities, and taking on board some tips and techniques to improve your use of time.

Delegation

Delegation is concerned with passing on authority and responsibility to different levels of staff within an organisation and is an important skill which you need to develop. It can be challenging if until your promotion to a management role, you had only been responsible for your own work and now you find yourself responsible for the work of others and need to allocate work to them.

Principle of delegation

Delegation means that a manager confers specific authority to a member of staff. It involves a dual responsibility. The person you have delegated the task to is responsible to you for doing the job, whereas you remain responsible for getting the job done. This is the principle of delegation and is the central process in all formal organisations (Mullins, 1996).

Some of the benefits of delegation

Delegating work appropriately to staff has many benefits, both for you as a manager and your staff. These include:

- creating more time for you to manage and to meet your managerial priorities
- allowing team members to gain specialist knowledge and skills through taking on responsibility for particular tasks
- staff becoming more motivated if they are able to gain more experience and develop new skills
- allocating work fairly among team members through the process of delegation
- decisions being made at the lowest level in the organisation that is compatible with efficiency.

The issue of trust and control

Trust and control have been described as the main issues of delegation by Charles Handy (1999). The trust is the trust your staff have in you as their manager, and control is the control that you have over the work of staff. Handy believes true delegation exists where there is delegation with trust and only the minimum of control. To achieve this requires a number of things.

- You must have confidence in your staff and believe that they can undertake the task you wish to delegate.

- Trust needs to be given to a member of staff, and you will have to wait and see whether your decision was warranted.

- Trust is reciprocal; you have to trust the member of staff and they have to trust you.

Delegation will depend on the situation, including:

- the complexity of the task to be undertaken

- your understanding of the level of risk involved

- your confidence in the skills and experience of the member of staff

- your self-confidence in your decision-making skills

- the pressures on you to get work done.

The extent to which you feel you are able to delegate work to members of your team will depend on these factors, but evidence from many studies suggests that managers often find delegation a difficult area of practice. You can develop your delegation skills by reflecting on your workload and whether you have created the correct balance of tasks, deciding on your preferred style of management (see **Chapter 5**) and developing an understanding of the skills of your staff team.

John Harris and Des Kelly suggest some useful starting points if you are doubtful about your delegation skills.

● Look back at your time management plans. Did they suggest priority areas that you need to focus on which could be improved by delegating more tasks to members of the team? Are you dealing with areas of work that stop you focusing on your priorities?

● Are you clear about the knowledge and skills of your team which could be utilised more fully in delegated tasks? Are there areas of work where members of staff perform well, or areas of work that could be done by staff following training?

Harris and Kelly caution that delegation does not produce results overnight, and that it may initially increase your workload – you may have to take risks and support staff. You may also feel it is 'quicker to do it yourself' and that you lose some control of aspects of the service. However, in the longer term it is a powerful means of achieving better results in the management of the service, both for you and your staff.

A systematic approach to delegation

It is useful to take a systematic approach to delegation and examine four basic questions.

1. What tasks could be performed better by your staff?

2. What opportunities exist for staff to develop their skills and extend their experience by taking on delegated tasks?

3. To whom should the delegated tasks be given?

4. What form of monitoring system is most appropriate?

If you are to delegate effectively to staff they should know what is expected of them, what standards of performance have to be achieved and how far they can exercise independent decision-making.

Managing your manager

An important skill that you need to develop as frontline manager is managing your manager. As John Harris and Des Kelly (1992) have described, the frontline manager's relationship with their manager is one where you have the choice to be passive and succumb to be managed, or to develop an active approach to managing your manager. They see the latter as part of your management role and one where both you and your manager can benefit from the development of a more active approach.

Understanding the world of your manager

Harris and Kelly maintain that one way to develop a more active approach is to understand the world of your manager: for example, your manager's role, their problems and needs and how you can help them achieve their aims. This recognises that you are both dependent on each other to achieve your respective goals. Some ways you can help your manager are to keep them informed by providing regular feedback and encouraging your manager to do the same for you. In keeping your manager informed, you enable them to understand your objectives and methods of achieving them.

Gaining respect

You can gain your manager's respect, and in turn gain greater autonomy, through your actions. These include: being punctual for meetings, ensuring reports are completed on time, anticipating tasks that need doing and having a relevant agenda when you meet with your manager.

Tactics

In developing your relationship with your manager, cultivate those areas of your work where you value your manager's involvement. These can be areas where you welcome challenges that can help you develop or refine your thinking or where you want to test out or clarify issues. If you have battles with your manager, try to choose the battleground carefully and seek clarity and consistency around what you expect your manager to do.

ACTIVITY

A way of checking your relationship with your manager is to complete the checklist below. Circle the numbers on the scale which you feel most clearly describe your relationship.

Does not keep me in the picture	1 2 3 4 5 6 7	Keeps me in the picture
Has vague or ambiguous objectives	1 2 3 4 5 6 7	Has clear objectives
Refuses to listen to my views	1 2 3 4 5 6 7	Is prepared to listen to my views
Not interested in my development	1 2 3 4 5 6 7	Interested in my development
Inconsistent in his/her policies	1 2 3 4 5 6 7	Consistent in his/her policies
Fails to represent my views	1 2 3 4 5 6 7	Represents my views
Unprepared to take decisions	1 2 3 4 5 6 7	Prepared to take decisions
Cannot count on his/her support	1 2 3 4 5 6 7	Can count on his/her support
Takes credit for my contribution	1 2 3 4 5 6 7	Gives credit to my contribution
Unable to respect him/her	1 2 3 4 5 6 7	Able to respect him/her
Does not take an interest in my work	1 2 3 4 5 6 7	Takes an interest in my work
Overloads me with work	1 2 3 4 5 6 7	Does not overload me
Fails to provide opportunities and challenges	1 2 3 4 5 6 7	Provides opportunities and challenges
Interferes with my work	1 2 3 4 5 6 7	Does not interfere with my work
Not available to see me	1 2 3 4 5 6 7	Available to see me

Now total the score (105 maximum). Does your score reflect your experience of your relationship with your manager?

(Harris & Kelly, 1992)

eg

What sort of relationship do you want with your manager? This is a statement from a team leader:

I need them to:

- do what they say

- not avoid me or start 'ducking and diving'

- give support

- give me answers

- be consistent

- relate to me how I want to relate to my team

I ensure that:

- I keep them informed, for example when complaints are coming through or there's major expenditure coming up

- they get no nasty surprises

- they are kept informed about difficult cases

- they are kept informed about morale in the team.

Managing pressure

The pressures on managers grow as more and more tasks are devolved to the front line and the range of responsibilities increases. Frontline managers often describe their work in terms of constant pressure and of not being able to complete any task satisfactorily. Although a certain amount of pressure can be stimulating, when it becomes too great it can easily turn into stress and can impair your effectiveness as a frontline manager.

John Harris and Des Kelly (1992) describe stress as an occupational hazard in social care which is likely to affect everyone at some point. Social care has some features which make stress more likely. These include:

- the relentless nature of human services

- the emotional demands of the work

- the undermining of self-worth by external criticism
- the exposed position of leadership in the service.

Stress occurs when the demands and the pressures of the work and non-work exceed the mechanisms we have for coping. Alan Barlow (1990) identifies categories of potential stress, including:

The job itself

- too much work to do
- too little work to do
- having to work long and unsocial hours
- too much or too little variety in the work
- poor physical working conditions
- time pressures and deadlines
- factors outside your control
- changes in working practices and systems

Your role in the organisation

- no clear objectives
- inadequate information about the role
- lack of power and influence
- personal beliefs conflicting with those of the organisation
- unclear expectations from your line manager
- conflicting tasks and demands
- inability to delegate
- being constantly available
- having to make difficult decisions
- practitioner and manager demands/conflicts

Your work relationships

- managing and supervising the work of staff
- lack of support from the team
- feeling isolated
- lack of positive feedback from your line manager
- personality clashes
- poor relationship with staff

Organisational climate

- inadequate guidance and support from line manager
- lack of consultation and communication
- staff shortages/high turnover rates
- inadequate feedback on performance
- insufficient resources to work with
- poor morale or organisational climate
- demands from services users/carers/pressure groups
- pace and complexity of change

Work/domestic interface

- taking work home
- not being able to 'switch off' at home
- spouse's/partner's attitude to your work
- demands work makes on your home life
- absence of emotional support
- few activities outside work
- putting your career ahead of your home life.

However, there are certain stress reducing strategies you can adopt to combat these:

- **problem solving:** taking action to reduce stress by tackling the problem
- **tension reduction:** lowering damaging arousal through relaxation, play, exercise or hobbies
- **positive thinking:** recognising destructive self-critical evaluation and destructive self-references
- **self-disclosure:** sharing your feelings informally with family, friends or colleagues, or formally with professional counsellors
- **assertive responses:** direct, straightforward expression of your opinions, beliefs, values or ideas. Avoiding aggressive or non-assertive responses
- **support:** developing a group of people who are willing to help you through stressful situations
- **stress monitoring:** being aware when tension builds up and of events or situations which trigger stressful responses
- **looking after yourself:** monitoring your health and keeping fit. Avoiding dependency on alcohol or smoking when stressed.

Action planning can also help. When action planning, think about the following points:

1. Areas which cause me greatest stress are...

2. Things I can do to manage my stress are...

3. Help and support that would I need in managing my stress...

The inner and outer game of management

Finally in this chapter on effectiveness in the management role it is useful to reflect on some ideas from the influential management thinker Peter Drucker (1974). Drucker has described one of the most important aspects of establishing yourself as a manager as linked to what he describes as the 'inner and outer game'.

The **outer game** is all those tasks and attendant skills which characterise management and the new role, such as allocating work, ensuring high quality standards of practice and supporting the work of individuals and teams.

On the other hand, the **inner game** is more complex and demanding because it is about managing your own self-esteem so that you derive satisfaction from undertaking management activities, including feeling comfortable with the authority of the management role and the responsibilities concerned with controlling staff and making difficult decisions. You also need to be able to manage the need to be liked in a way that does not interfere with performing the management role effectively, particularly where you have to make difficult decisions about resources and disappoint staff when you have to refuse their requests.

KEY POINTS

○ Understanding the strategic objectives for your service and how these relate to the specific objectives for your team can be a useful starting point for developing your priorities in the frontline role.

○ Managing your time is important so that you can create space to do the right things based on your priorities. Spending some time analysing how you use your time and adopting some simple techniques can be a great help in making better use of this finite resource.

○ Delegation is the basis of all management and a skill you need to develop. Developing these skills will lead you to examine your management activities and discover what can be delegated to team members, thereby enhancing their skills and creating opportunities for you to concentrate on your priority tasks.

○ Understanding your relationship with your manager and how you manage that relationship can help improve your effectiveness.

○ Frontline managers work under constant pressure. Understanding what stresses you and how you can manage your stress is a vital part of surviving the management role.

○ Understanding the 'inner game' of management can be helpful in feeling more positive about yourself in your relationships with others and in situations where you have to make difficult decisions.

Leadership

Introduction

All social care agencies place considerable faith in recruiting managers who have, or can develop, leadership qualities. A cursory glance at the advertisements for frontline management posts in social services departments confirms the wish to appoint people who are expected to 'lead developments', 'demonstrate leadership qualities', 'lead their teams' and more recently 'lead the transformation of the service'. These advertisements suggest that organisations have an expectation that leadership is an essential aspect of managing at all levels in the service, not just at the apex of the organisation.

Changing perspectives on leadership

Leadership is traditionally associated with the great charismatic and heroic figures from political and military history. In more modern organisational contexts it usually involves the authority-based direction of staff by senior managers.

With the growth of more contemporary ideas about organisational development, particularly the continuing devolvement of responsibility to the front line and the empowerment of staff, leadership qualities are seen as important at all levels of the organisation.

A further contrast with the past is the view that managers can develop their leadership skills though training and development, and that leadership is no longer an innate quality that resides in particular individuals.

ACTIVITY

Can you identify a manager you have worked with who you felt demonstrated leadership qualities?

1. What was it about that person that led you to see him/her as a leader?

....

....

....

2. What were some of their personal characteristics which suggested leadership qualities?

....

....

....

When you have completed this activity you might find it interesting to compare it with the following list.

eg

Post-qualifying social work students suggested some of the positive attributes they valued in frontline managers who demonstrated leadership qualities:

- a vision of where the team is going
- a good communicator
- an ideas person
- enthusiastic
- approachable
- works alongside people and acknowledges their contribution
- doesn't take the credit for the work of others
- supportive and takes an interest in team members
- values team members
- delegates work appropriately.

Some of these attributes could be considered qualities found in any effective manager. However students suggested that an emphasis on vision, suggesting ideas and being an enthusiastic communicator set managers apart and indicated leadership qualities. When we come to examine **Transactional and transformational leadership** (see **page 57**) we will recognise a number of these qualities again.

> 'In developing my own style I knew what sort of leader I wanted to be. I based it on two of my previous managers whom I admired. They were clear and consistent, you knew where you stood with them, they were available and supportive and thought things through in a professional way. You felt safe with them.'
>
> Team leader

Leader or manager?

Often the terms 'manager' and 'leader' are used interchangeably, with Rosemary Stewart (1997) stating that 'leader' is a term that often has more appeal in modern organisations. Nevertheless there are differences. Management is essentially about people with responsibility for the work of others and what they actually do operationally, whereas leadership is concerned with the ability to influence others towards the achievement of particular organisational goals and can be seen in the attributes of a vision of the team's direction in the example above.

Different approaches to leadership: the 'best fit' approach

Charles Handy (1999) has described a range of factors which confront the leader and which need to be taken into consideration:

- the leader's preferred style of operating and his or her personal characteristics
- the staff and their preferred style of leadership
- the task, the job to be done, its objectives and the techniques to be used to complete the task
- the environment, including the organisational setting of the leader, the group and the importance of the task.

This approach suggests that there is no one 'right' style of leadership, but that leadership is most effective when the requirements of the leader, the staff and the task fit together.

Structuring and supporting

Charles Handy has described the different leadership approaches on a scale ranging from tight to flexible. This has many similarities to the styles of leadership behaviour described by Robert Tannerbaum and Warren Schmidt (1973) who describe the continuum of leadership style as operating between 'boss-centred leadership' and 'group centred leadership'.

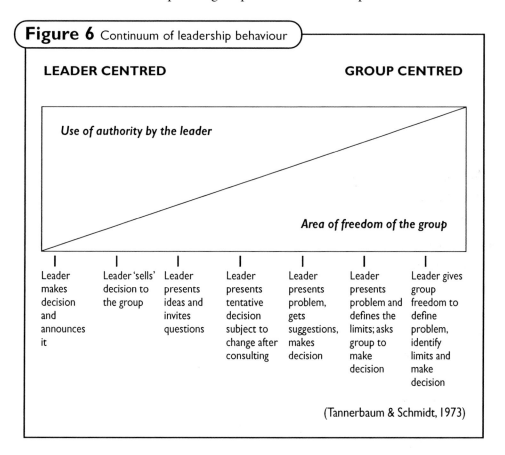

Figure 6 Continuum of leadership behaviour

LEADER CENTRED   **GROUP CENTRED**

Use of authority by the leader

Area of freedom of the group

| Leader makes decision and announces it | Leader 'sells' decision to the group | Leader presents ideas and invites questions | Leader presents tentative decision subject to change after consulting | Leader presents problem, gets suggestions, makes decision | Leader presents problem and defines the limits; asks group to make decision | Leader gives group freedom to define problem, identify limits and make decision |

(Tannerbaum & Schmidt, 1973)

Using Handy's approach, the tight end of the continuum suggests a 'structuring' approach where staff have a preference for the leader having more control over their work, and where the manager likes to control and make decisions and initiate activity. This is in contrast to the flexible end of the continuum which is 'supportive', where the manager consults with individuals and the team and encourages participation in decision-making.

ACTIVITY

1. What is your preferred leadership style?

....

....

....

2. Identify a situation where you found yourself at a particular point along the continuum of leadership behaviour.

....

....

....

3. What factors in the situation led you to adopt a particular style?

....

....

....

Influences on leadership

Handy has also described a number of factors that influence leadership.

Your own attitude to the leadership role

This includes:

● your own leadership inclinations, how comfortable you are with the idea of being a leader and whether you tend towards a task-focused or people-focused approach

- your views about your team and your confidence in them
- your tolerance of ambiguity
- your own view of yourself as a leader and what is required to develop the service
- how far your style of leadership matches the culture of the organisation.

The attitudes of your staff

These include:

- what they want from you as their leader
- the attitudes and needs of the people in your team
- how they perceive your leadership
- how far they feel confident in you
- the support they expect from you
- your relationships with staff
- the extent to which you are able to establish trust, mutual respect and rapport with the team and show concern, warmth and consideration for team members.

The organisational situation

This includes:

- the organisational context in which you and the team are located
- the strategic intent of the organisation – what it is trying to achieve and what is needed to deliver the vision
- the purpose of your unit within the larger organisation
- the values of the organisation.

The influence of culture on your leadership style

Organisational culture has been described as the set of values, norms and beliefs which are reflected in different structures and systems. Culture is also affected by the history of the organisation, the current climate, the work it is engaged in and the kind of people who work in the organisation. Your leadership style will be influenced by the culture of the organisation and other people's expectations of you (Handy, 1999).

ACTIVITY

Can you describe the culture of your organisation?

Note: You may find that the wider organisation is a mixture of two or three different cultures and that there is a difference between the organisational culture and that of your team.

1. Is it a culture which is strongly authoritarian, where hierarchy and power are used to control the organisation – what has been described as a 'power culture'?

    ....

    ....

2. Is it a culture which requires conformity to prescribed tasks and procedures – what has been described as a 'role culture'?

    ....

    ....

3. Is it one where the organisation encourages staff to work together to solve problems and is task-oriented for achievement purposes – an 'achievement culture'?

    ....

    ....

4. Is it an organisation where concern for the individual is uppermost and openness and co-operation are key values – the 'support culture'?

    ....

    ....

ACTIVITY

Consider these questions, writing down your ideas on a sheet of paper.

1. Can you identify the dominant culture of your organisation?

2. Does the culture of your team differ from the wider organisational culture?

3. What does this suggest in terms of how you need to manage your team?

Whatever the culture (and it is likely to be a mix of different elements), it will suggest ways in which your leadership style will need to adapt to the cultural expectations of the organisation, and also to the sub-culture of your team.

Transactional and transformational leadership: two approaches to leadership

James Burns (1978) discusses leadership in terms of two fundamental types of leader – the transactional and the transformational.

The transactional leader

Transactional leadership describes those important activities necessary for maintaining routine service operations, with the emphasis on detailed planning, organising staffing, controlling and monitoring day-to-day operations and problem-solving. This form of leadership is associated with the 'command and control' functions of management and is based on the 'contract' with mutual expectations on the part of the leader and the led. It is a form of leadership which emphasises compliance and acceptance of direction.

The transformational leader

That staff increasingly expect to be 'led' by leaders who share power and responsibility and managers expect to gain the collaboration and commitment of staff through shared commitment to the values and the purpose of the service means a different form of leadership is required.

Transformational leadership is a term that has now become common currency in many public services. Its emphasis is on creating the conditions for commitment to fundamental change in services, based on vision and innovation. Transformational leadership is essentially concerned with the way leaders involve their staff in transforming themselves and the way they work. Emphasis is on inspiring staff around shared values and developing a purposeful approach to the development of the service.

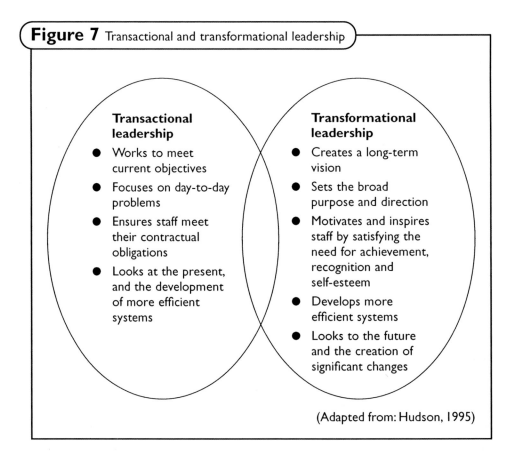

Figure 7 Transactional and transformational leadership

Transactional leadership

- Works to meet current objectives
- Focuses on day-to-day problems
- Ensures staff meet their contractual obligations
- Looks at the present, and the development of more efficient systems

Transformational leadership

- Creates a long-term vision
- Sets the broad purpose and direction
- Motivates and inspires staff by satisfying the need for achievement, recognition and self-esteem
- Develops more efficient systems
- Looks to the future and the creation of significant changes

(Adapted from: Hudson, 1995)

The descriptions in the diagram above should suggest the style of leadership you should be developing. Of course, there are still areas of management that require a transactional approach, but the growing demands on the frontline manager suggest a much more dynamic process that develops a reciprocal leader–follower relationship. This two-way process is used to influence the individual's and the organisation's performance.

This means that as leader you need to think about the future and work to achieve what is best for the service and its staff. It means working alongside staff, communicating the vision for the service and supporting and enhancing their performance through a commitment to shared goals.

Attributes of effective leadership

Ruth Wheatley and Cathy Smith (1995) have listed the key attributes that various management writers associate with leadership, including:

- an attitude of constant learning
- the development of confidence and high self-esteem
- a willingness to question and listen to answers
- a capacity for building relationships
- an appreciation of other people's work
- an ability to develop leadership in others
- innovation and initiative
- the capacity to develop a vision of the future
- an ability to communicate well at every level
- integrity and trustworthiness
- the capacity to trust others
- coaching and counselling skills.

Although Wheatley and Smith caution that this may appear like a 'wish list', these attributes do seem to correlate closely with what social workers and managers say about colleagues who demonstrate leadership qualities. What is interesting about this list is its similarity to the earlier list created by students. It seems that effective leadership centres around a number of personal qualities which are recognised and valued by a wide range of staff.

KEY POINTS

○ Your leadership style will depend on the situation and will be influenced by how you see your role, how you see your staff and the particular requirements imposed by the work situation.

○ No single style is appropriate for all situations. Effective leadership is best achieved through adapting your style to suit the situation and the competencies of your team members.

○ Your style of leadership will be influenced by the interplay of a number of factors, including: your own approach to your role, the staff you have to manage and their skills, the task to be achieved, and the culture of the organisation.

○ A more participative and supportive style of leadership has been found to result in a higher degree of satisfaction and greater involvement of staff teams. An understanding of the feelings of staff and their needs and expectations is seen as an essential ingredient.

○ Recognise that some people need (or prefer to be) directed and to have their work structured – particularly when they are not ready to take on full responsibility or do not value independent decision-making. This may be so particularly in cases where the work is repetitive or routine.

○ Managing at the front line is no longer just about implementing policies decided by senior managers. You are now expected to lead and develop your service.

Managing individuals

Introduction

Staff who responded to my survey stated that a manager's understanding of the needs of staff and his/her relationship with them is one of the most important factors in the success of a team. As frontline manager, this means you will need to create an environment where your relationship with staff is one of developing trust and support, where you are able to listen to them, reflect on their situation and respond flexibly to their needs.

You need to provide support for staff, recognising the demands frontline work makes on them and providing regular supervision where they have space to discuss their work in a supportive environment. At the same time you are faced with an increasing range of demands related to performance and these will need to be communicated to staff. In your role of monitoring individual staff performance you will have to be certain that they are meeting departmental requirements, and if not, take appropriate action.

eg

In a survey of post-qualifying students' expectations of their manager, the following statements were listed:

- to be encouraging, guiding and supportive
- to offer advice in difficult situations
- to provide regular, good quality supervision

Continued...

eg continued

- to give feedback on performance
- to monitor performance
- an 'open door policy' so I can talk to my manager when I need to
- to hold regular team meetings
- a 'person's person', approachable and with a sense of humour
- to be in touch with the reality of practice
- to help me develop my role and career
- to keep me informed of changes in the department and the team
- to be loyal and honest.

These statements provide a useful basis for thinking about the areas that you need to develop as a frontline manager if you are to respond sensitively to the needs of staff. We will now examine some of the important areas in managing individuals.

Supporting staff

Support from the frontline manager was the most frequently quoted statement in the survey of post-qualifying students and managers of residential services. So much of the frontline management role is about establishing relationships with members of your team that are open and trusting in order to create a climate to assess their strengths and needs, and identify ways of helping them develop their skills through supervision, appraisal and training.

A team leader, describing his former manager, said:

'It's (the manager) being human and developing a good relationship with staff, building a cohesive group, making people feel important and acknowledging that the job is difficult, but you're with the team, working together'.

Understanding motivation

A major part of your responsibility is to understand and identify what helps motivate your staff. This should enable you to develop practice opportunities and working conditions which enable them to perform well. There will be some factors which influence motivation that are outside your control. Nevertheless you will still have scope and influence to increase motivation, particularly in matching activities to needs so that staff are more satisfied.

What motivates a person is a result of a combination of factors, including their needs, the incentives provided and their perceptions of the organisation. Ideally a person's needs should be matched by incentives provided by the organisation. What motivates a person is highly subjective and what satisfies one person may not be satisfying to another. It is this subjectivity that can make managing individuals a difficult process.

Motivation is also complicated in social care agencies by the deeper motives of staff who work in these departments. Mike Hudson (1995) has suggested that staff tend to have strong ideals and attach great importance to job satisfaction. Financial rewards are less important, and the content of the job is seen as an important part of the compensation package.

Importance of the psychological contract

All employees have a legal contract with their organisation, but Laurie Mullins (1996) introduces the idea of the unstated contract – something he describes as the **psychological contract**. This is not a written document, but a series of mutual expectations and satisfactions of need arising from the person–organisation relationship.

This contract is seen to have an important influence on people's behaviour in organisations.

The individual's expectations

- Safe working environment
- Job security
- Challenging and satisfying work
- Equitable personnel policies
- Genuine participation in decisions which affect them
- Opportunities for personal development and career progression
- Being treated with respect
- Understanding and consideration when experiencing personal problems

The organisation's expectations

- Accept the corporate goals of the organisation
- Work to achieve organisational objectives
- Uphold the image and reputation of the organisation
- Show loyalty to the organisation
- Not to betray positions of trust

Balancing the expectations

Charles Handy (1999) also discusses the psychological contract and believes that it is not seen identically by both parties – the organisation is likely to have an all-embracing view whereas the individual might not. This can lead to the individual feeling exploited and the organisation believing that the staff lack commitment.

Handy sees a **co-operative contract** as ideal. In the co-operative contract, the individual identifies with the organisation's goals and is committed to pursuing them. Where this happens, staff are involved to a greater extent in the identification of goals and have discretion in how they are achieved. (This a reciprocal relationship where the management of the organisation devolves more responsibility.) Handy sees this approach to the psychological contract becoming more common, although he cautions that organisations can be surprised and offended when these approaches are rebuffed. Goals that are meaningful to managers are not necessarily viewed in the same way by staff, and sharing responsibility for goals as well as decisions about achieving them is not something all staff want to participate in.

ACTIVITY

Consider the following points, writing down your ideas on a separate sheet of paper.

Expectations

- What are your expectations of your organisation?

- Are you clear about your organisation's expectations of you?

- Is there a match or mismatch between the expectations?

- What does your example suggest in terms of your staff's expectations?

Motivation

Reflect on your own motivation.

- What motivates you?

- What demotivates you?

Making sense of motivation

Expectations by members of staff about the organisation have important implications for motivation. Although there are many theories of motivation, for the purposes of this manual three areas have proved helpful to frontline managers. These include: needs theories, incentive theories and job design.

Needs theory

Probably the most popular theory is **Maslow's hierarchy of needs**. It highlights the importance of needs in energising behaviour. Need fulfilment is seen as an important factor in behaviour and the relationship between the individual and their needs.

Maslow's theory is well known and states that lower level needs must be satisfied before higher level ones become dominant, with the individual striving to satisfy evolving higher order needs. It is possible to relate Maslow's level of needs to the work situation at each stage in the hierarchy. This is represented diagrammatically.

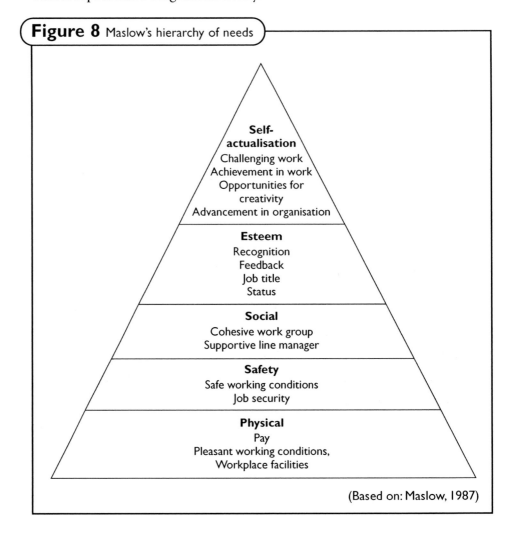

Figure 8 Maslow's hierarchy of needs

Self-actualisation
Challenging work
Achievement in work
Opportunities for creativity
Advancement in organisation

Esteem
Recognition
Feedback
Job title
Status

Social
Cohesive work group
Supportive line manager

Safety
Safe working conditions
Job security

Physical
Pay
Pleasant working conditions,
Workplace facilities

(Based on: Maslow, 1987)

ACTIVITY

1. What does the diagram tell you about the relationship between levels in the hierarchy and motivational factors in the workplace?

....

....

....

2. Drawing on Maslow's theory of motivation, can you identify where it would be possible to increase the motivation of staff?

....

....

....

Two factor theory

These are mainly the theories of **Frederick Herzberg** (1968). Herzberg argues that two sets of factors – the motivation factor and the hygiene factor – work in combination to provide the incentives or disincentives to the application of greater effort to work.

When present, the satisfiers or 'motivators' lead to job satisfaction. These factors are said to affect the person's degree of satisfaction and are seen as important for motivation.

Hygiene or maintenance factors (analogous to the medical term 'preventative') serve to prevent dissatisfaction. Where they are present they reduce job dissatisfaction, although they are said not actually to motivate. They relate to Maslow's lower order or primary needs.

These are represented diagrammatically (see **figure 9**, overleaf).

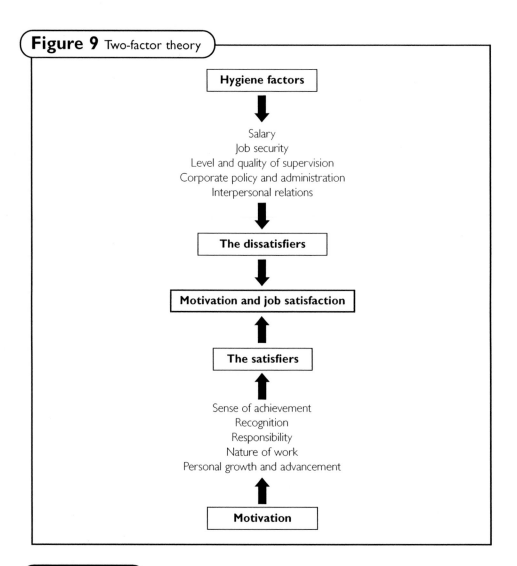

Figure 9 Two-factor theory

Hygiene factors

Salary
Job security
Level and quality of supervision
Corporate policy and administration
Interpersonal relations

The dissatisfiers

Motivation and job satisfaction

The satisfiers

Sense of achievement
Recognition
Responsibility
Nature of work
Personal growth and advancement

Motivation

ACTIVITY

With Figure 9 in mind, answer the following questions, noting down your ideas on a sheet of paper.

1. What does Herzberg's theory suggest about motivation in your organisation?

2. Are there hygiene factors that could be improved to reduce job dissatisfaction?

3. Are there job motivators that could be improved? This is an area where you have more scope to influence the individual's motivation.

Job design and enrichment

The concept of job design and job enrichment is based on motivation theories that have proved useful to frontline managers in suggesting ideas for improving staff's satisfaction with their work. Job design and enrichment is based on the work of Richard Hackman and Greg Oldham (1980), where restructuring work and providing job enrichment to make work more interesting and challenging are seen as the basis for greater job satisfaction.

They view job enrichment in terms of five core dimensions:

- **skill variety** – the job has a range of activities and involves staff in using a range of skills and talents

- **task identity** – the opportunity to complete a whole job with a visible outcome

- **task significance** – the job has a meaningful impact on other people, both inside and outside the organisation

- **autonomy** – the extent to which the job provides the opportunity for autonomy, independence and discretion in planning and deciding how to undertake it

- **feedback** – the extent to which work activities result in direct and clear information on the effectiveness of job performance.

These core characteristics are said to create three psychological states:

- work is experienced as meaningful

- staff experience responsibility for the outcomes of their work

- there is knowledge of the outcomes of work activities.

This research would suggest that the work situations staff will find most satisfying and rewarding are those that provide them with:

- opportunities to satisfy job content

- a sense of achievement and recognition

- authority and responsibility

- growth, advancement and self-development

- variety, creativity and challenge.

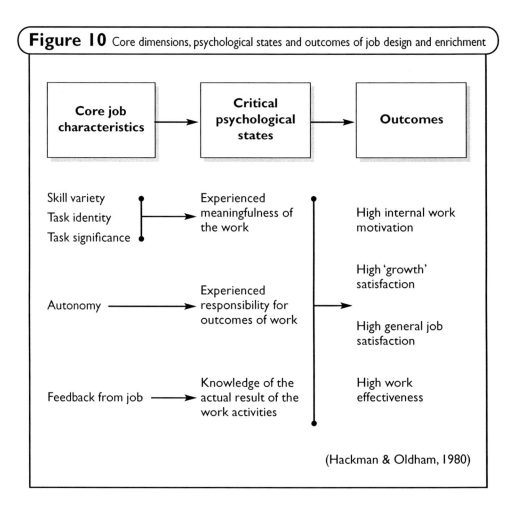

Figure 10 Core dimensions, psychological states and outcomes of job design and enrichment

(Hackman & Oldham, 1980)

Laurie Mullins (1996) cautions that although the job content factors can be satisfying, if the job context factors, organisational policies, interpersonal relationships, work conditions, salary and supervision deteriorate and cause a climate of dissatisfaction and tension, this will affect the individual's performance.

It should also be remembered that not all staff will seek a more enriched, challenging or demanding job. Some staff may not wish to accept greater responsibility or autonomy and may prefer more routine work and a higher level of direction and control by the manager. Understanding staff's individual perceptions of their work will help you create the conditions in which different needs can be met.

eg

Post-qualifying management students produced the following list of factors that increased their motivation:

- clear policies and guidance on related practice issues

- positive values and attitudes in the team

- supervision and support

- adequate resources

- training and development opportunities

- good communication

- consistent management approach.

Combining theories of motivation

Although there are competing theories about motivation which reflect its complexity, combining the elements of different theories suggests strategies for increasing staff motivation levels.

- The psychological contract is a useful concept in understanding the match between individual members of staff and the organisation's expectations.

- Many motives are likely to influence staff's behaviour. The theories suggest where you need to direct your attention when thinking about how to motivate staff.

- Try to match what each member of staff wants from their work with what the organisation has to offer.

- Different people want different things from their work, and what motivates you will not necessarily be the same as that which motivates your staff. However, reflecting on your own needs and expectations in relation to the job and to the organisation can offer insights into motivation issues.

Supervision

A recurring theme in reports on the needs of frontline staff is the central importance of professional supervision (see for example, Stevenson and Parsloe, 1978 and more recently Kearney, 1999). Phyllida Parsloe and Olive Stevenson originally argued, and it still holds good today, that supervision is important for two reasons: first as a means of establishing the accountability of worker to the organisation and second, to promote the worker's development as a professional. Seen in this way supervision is both part of the management and the professional practice systems and provides the links between the two.

Supervision remains crucial to supporting high quality practice, but has been beset by a number of problems. These include the growth of managerialism in services that emphasised more directive forms of management, the increasing number of tasks devolved to frontline managers which diverted them from this essential activity, and questions about the role of supervision in modern management practice.

Organisational issues

At a time when the demands on staff continue to grow there are many issues facing supervisors. Tony Morrison (1996) has listed some of the typical problems that affect supervision. These include:

- lack of agency policies
- lack of time and space
- interruptions to supervision
- supervision that is reactive rather than planned
- inadequate recording of supervision
- focus on workload control and current crisis.

eg

Discussions with staff working in residential and day services confirm that many of the problems identified by Tony Morrison are familiar to staff. They suggested a number of changes that would improve the quality of supervision:

- maintaining regular supervision sessions and only cancelling as a last resort for genuine reasons

- ensuring sessions are not interrupted by telephone calls and other callers

- making a contractual agreement on the purposes of supervision and how it can help staff improve their practice

- supervisors providing helpful feedback on practice

- supervisors being willing to give advice and demonstrate a real commitment to practice

- focusing on outcomes for the user rather than managerial monitoring of performance in a narrow sense

- ensuring there is a willingness to examine the complex and demanding aspects of practice, particularly those which engender stress.

A definition and model of supervision

The main concerns reflect to some extent the need to clarify the purpose of supervision and to confirm its importance though organisational policies which legitimise its role and provide managers with confidence in undertaking it.

Tony Morrison quotes a definition of supervision:

'Supervision is a process in which one worker is given responsibility to work with another worker in order to meet organisational, professional and personal objectives. These are competence, accountable performance, continuing professional development and personal support.'

(Morrison, 1996)

This is helpful in clarifying supervision as:

- an activity located in the context of a clearly defined relationship

- an ongoing process

- possessing a number of objectives, including organisational, professional and personal.

The purpose of supervision is to:

- ensure the worker is clear about roles and responsibilities

- ensure the worker meets the agency's objectives

- ensure quality of service to users and carers

- support a suitable climate for practice

- support professional development

- reduce stress

- ensure the worker has the resources to do the job.

    (Morrison, 1996)

eg

Staff from residential services consulted for this manual identified a number of improvements they would like to see:

- supervision conducted in a relaxed and friendly atmosphere

- sessions booked and not changed at short notice by the manager

- sessions not interrupted

- supervisors putting items on the supervision agenda and not leaving it to the member of staff to develop the agenda each time

- recognition of the high emotional content of the work, with strategies for helping the member of staff manage this

- a better balance between service user issues and management issues

- more feedback please!

For managers who are uncertain about the supervision role, it can be helpful to have a model as the basis for action. Jacky Knapman and Tony Morrison (1998) describe the four main functions of supervision, which also draw on the work of Margaret Richards and Chris Payne (1990).

- **Managerial function** – this is concerned primarily with the overall performance of the worker and ensuring that their practice is in line with the agency's expectations and standards. Supervision in this function will focus on the roles and responsibilities of staff, their accountability and performance, and how well they are meeting the organisation's demands.

- **Development function** – this is concerned with enabling workers to assess their own skills and competence and develop these as appropriate. Supervision in this function will focus on exploring experiences which are the basis for learning, examining knowledge, values and attitudes, and identifying the workers' strengths and weaknesses in relation to practice. Feedback will be given on performance and training needs identified.

- **Supportive function** – where a safe and trusting relationship is shared between supervisor and worker to enable the worker to identify and deal with the personal impact of his or her work. Supervision in this function will focus on the discussion of feelings, exploration of emotional issues that may be blocking practice and dealing with stress.

- **Mediation function** – this function is concerned with feedback from the organisation to the individual and from the individual to the organisation. Here, supervision focuses on communication both up and down the organisation to provide the link between the worker and the wider organisation. It will focus specifically on organisational developments and changes and issues about resource constraints which are represented or negotiated on your behalf or on behalf of the team.

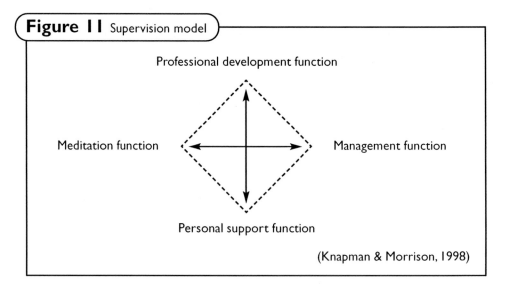

Figure 11 Supervision model

Professional development function

Meditation function

Management function

Personal support function

(Knapman & Morrison, 1998)

ACTIVITY

Preparing for supervision

As you take on responsibility for supervision it is helpful to use a checklist to assess your preparedness. This has been adapted from Peter Hawkins and Robin Shohet (1990):

1. Do you understand the purpose of supervision?

2. Do you understand the functions of supervision?

3. Have you explained the purpose of supervision to the worker?

4. Did you negotiate a mutually agreed contract?

5. Do you create a climate in supervision that is empathic, genuine and safe?

6. Do you manage the supervision session appropriately?

7. Do you record the supervision?

Group supervision

Although group supervision can be seen as a more economical or realistic alternative, it can also be seen in some situations as an inferior alternative to individual supervision. However, Veronica Coulshed (1990) suggests that one positive reason for choosing group supervision is that each member learns from other people's experiences. It can also be beneficial in changing the dynamic between supervisor and supervisees and enable other methods (eg role play, sculpting and case studies) to be used in place of the usual one-to-one discussion.

Similarly, Patricia Kearney (1999) discusses the need to move beyond the limited view of supervision as either confidential one-to-one sessions concentrating on the supervisee's personal development or checking procedural compliance. Instead, she suggests that supervision should be undertaken with the team examining the content of practice, the methods used and the processes workers engage in.

Kearney cautions that developing group supervision calls for management skills of a high order, and that frontline managers will need to develop their confidence to work with staff teams on practice issues. A combination of authority and autonomy is seen by Kearney as important for managers taking on this work.

'I always wanted to introduce supervision in the home care team as I'd experienced its beneficial role in my previous job. My team of staff is too big to enable me to supervise them individually so I had to go for group supervision. After some initial suspicion it seems to be working well and helpful to staff who are now working with much more dependent clients than in the past.'

Home care manager

Performance appraisal

Like supervision, staff appraisal is a method that is used to ensure that staff are clear about what is expected of them and that the organisation provides the resources and support to enable them to achieve agreed objectives. Whereas supervision is an ongoing process and deals with mainly short-term performance requirements (although there will be longer-term developmental goals), appraisal is normally part of an annual cycle of setting and reviewing performance targets against agreed objectives.

Benefits of appraisal

An effective appraisal system offers a number of potential benefits to both staff and the organisation:

- it can be used to identify the staff's strengths and weaknesses and what measures need to be put in place to enable the weaknesses to be addressed

- staff can use the appraisal interview to highlight problems which are affecting their performance

- staff can use the appraisal to discuss their ideas and expectations

- staff can receive feedback on their performance

- it can identify where staff have potential to take on more responsibility and for promotion

- it can help the managers with resource planning as changes in the workload of staff indicate areas needing additional resources.

The frontline manager and appraisal

With the devolvement of human resource management systems as part of organisational development, the frontline manager will be expected to conduct appraisal interviews. According to Charles Handy (1999) this can create difficulties in the multiple roles the manager plays in relation to the person being appraised. This can occur particularly in relation to some of the objectives of appraisal – for example, feedback on performance and helping staff plan work objectives and ways of achieving them. He also adds that managers usually get little training on how to conduct performance appraisals. Some of the reasons why appraisal is difficult include:

- staff do not like to admit to significant deficiencies, but without disclosure there is no commitment to dealing with them

- criticism of performance arouses defence mechanisms and does not improve performance

- the relationship of the line manager with the member of staff will affect the appraisal interview.

Handy also comments that the manager has to be judge and counsellor at the same time and this raises issues about the effectiveness of appraisal. For appraisal to be effective there are a number of requirements:

- the manager should keep comments about performance to specific instances, rather than general comments about performance

- the manager should be trusted and respected by the member of staff

- the manager should have a genuine liking for, and wish to help the member of staff

- the manager is regarded by the member of staff as helpful, facilitating and receptive to ideas and able to plan

- improved performance results from setting goals rather than criticising performance

- support should be given to the member of staff, and they should be encouraged to initiate the evaluation of their own performance as the basis for further goal setting.

KEY POINTS

- Support from frontline managers through an open and trusting relationship is highly valued by staff.

- Understanding motivation theories can help you understand staff's motivation and what you can do to increase motivation.

- Job enrichment theories can be helpful in creating conditions that lead to greater job satisfaction.

- Supervision, in its different forms, is crucial to supporting high quality practice.

- Performance appraisal is seen as important in organisations, but to undertake this work effectively requires you to understand some of the complexities of the role.

Managing poor performance

Introduction

Poor performance is one of the most difficult areas for the frontline manager, and was mentioned frequently by managers as an area that generated high levels of anxiety and frustration. Comments made by a number of managers suggested that this was an area of practice where they often felt on their own with little back-up from line managers or human resource departments. The newly appointed manager can find management of the most competent staff demanding, but managing in a situation where staff are clearly not competent or motivated can be one of the most difficult management problems they will face.

Poor performance

Causes of poor performance

Poor performance can be caused by a wide range of factors. Your responsibility as manager is to identify with the member of staff the causes of the poor performance so that corrective action can be taken. Some of the causes could include:

- lack of clarity about the range of responsibilities
- lack of, or poor induction
- irregular or poor quality supervision
- relationship between yourself and the worker
- the worker's relationship with peers

- mismatch between the culture of the organisation and the worker

- lack of resources to do the job

- lack of skills to do the job

- personal problems impeding performance

- poor motivation.

Taking action early

It is important to identify poor performance at an early stage before it causes major problems for the quality of service and has an effect on other team members. Managers spoke of the importance of promoting service standards and regular supervision as two ways of being much clearer about performance standards and making it easier to know when to discuss poor performance.

> 'Poor performance is something I try to address in supervision. It needs to be addressed early before things get difficult. It's been difficult dealing with it (poor performance) when it's been ignored or swept under the carpet by a previous manager. It's crucial to keep detailed records of the problem and what you have said to the member of staff as you will need them to back you up later if you can't resolve it at an earlier stage.'
>
> **Team leader**

Addressing poor performance

Good practice is important when dealing with poor performance. Kevin Ford and Sarah Hargreaves (1991) suggest the following steps in tackling poor performance:

- when meeting with a member of staff whose performance is poor, plan ahead and think through what you will say and how you will say it

- share your concerns with the member of staff at an early stage – don't let the situation develop to the stage where it is impossible to take corrective action

- focus on the facts
- act assertively, not aggressively or non-assertively
- explain why you are raising the issue
- ask for a response – ask the member of staff for their view of what has happened and why
- identify the causes of the poor performance with the member of staff
- plan together to correct the poor performance, setting short-term objectives
- agree a date to review progress.

Preparing for the meeting with a member of staff: using the DESC script

Many managers commented on their anxiety about how they would actually communicate the problem to a member of staff. The use of the DESC script technique can be useful as a way of helping you think through what to say, to be clear and forceful and to describe the problem in a non-judgemental way.

- **Describe (D)** what the member of staff is doing that is creating the problem.
- **Express (E)** why the behaviour is a problem – for you as the manager and for the organisation.
- **Specify (S)** what the member of staff should be doing instead.
- **Consequences (C)** of either succeeding or failing to change the problem behaviour.

The presentation should be thought through before meeting with the member of staff. It can also help to write the script out and practise it beforehand. This provides a mental checklist when you actually confront the member of staff.

What a member of staff hears

A useful way of checking out your presentation is to ask yourself the following questions:

- if I was the person receiving this script, would I be clear about what I am doing that is a problem, why there is a problem and what my manager wants me to do about it?
- are the statements by the manager likely to put me on the defensive?

'One of the most difficult parts of my job has been dealing with a member of staff whose poor performance is damaging work with clients and morale in the team. In spite of numerous requests for help I've had little support. I'm expected to manage the situation even though its been going on for years. I seem to get no help from headquarters.'

Manager of a residential service

Not dealing with poor performance on your own

The experience of this frontline manager confirms Patricia Kearney's (1999) view that frontline managers are often expected to contain persistent poor performance because departments do not wish to engage in protracted action to resolve the situation. Rather than the poorly performing staff member's competence being questioned, it is the frontline manager whose competence is questioned. More support from line managers and human resource department staff is essential if frontline managers are not to be left unsupported and to deal with poor performance on their own.

ACTIVITY

If you have a member of staff whose performance concerns you, what action do you take?

- Raise the issue of performance in supervision and appraisal meetings?
- Keep detailed records of your discussion with the member of staff?
- Discuss with your line manager?
- Consult the human resources department?

Disciplinary procedures

Where poor performance persists in spite of action to correct it, it may be necessary to use disciplinary procedures. These procedures should be seen as a means of correcting and improving standards of performance, not of administering punishment. As a frontline manager you will be expected to initiate these procedures when necessary and take part in disciplinary hearings. This manual does not deal with disciplinary procedures as these should only be taken in consultation with your line manager and the human resources department where staff have expertise in these procedures. Part of preparing yourself for the frontline management role means establishing what is expected of you and the limits to your delegated responsibilities in relation to disciplinary procedures.

KEY POINTS

- Dealing with members of staff whose performance is poor is a major area of anxiety to many frontline managers.

- It is important to establish the causes of poor performance before taking action.

- Take action at the earliest stage possible once you have identified the causes.

- Think through how you will confront a member of staff who is performing poorly. Use well established procedures.

- Don't deal with poor performance on your own. Draw on the expertise of the human resources staff in your organisation.

- Be clear about your responsibilities in relation to disciplinary procedures.

Managing teams

Introduction

Much of the work of social services departments is undertaken by teams, with staff appointed to work together to achieve organisational objectives. One of your roles as frontline manager is to lead your team and release its potential to enable the team to achieve results greater than the sum of its parts. To do this successfully means being aware of those factors which influence the performance of teams and how you can improve teamworking.

Definitions of teams

There are numerous definitions of what constitutes a team. For example:

> 'a group that shares a common purpose and recognises that it needs the efforts of every one of its members to achieve this.'
>
> **(Barrett, 1987)**

or

> 'a group in which the individuals have a common aim and in which the jobs and skills of each member fit in with those of others'
>
> **(Babbington-Smith & Farrell, 1979)**

John Adair (1987) has suggested that a work group is likely to have the following characteristics:

- a definable membership
- a group consciousness, with members having a collective perception of unity and identification with each other

- a shared purpose, with members having the same common task or goal

- interdependence, with members needing each others' help to accomplish the task

- interaction, with members communicating and influencing each other

- a unitary way of behaving, with the group working as a single entity.

Purposes of groups in organisations

According to Charles Handy (1999), groups within organisations have different but related purposes.

The organisation's purposes include:

- **the distribution of work** – bringing together a set of skills, talents and responsibilities and matching them to particular duties

- **the management and control of work** – allowing work to be organised and controlled by team members with responsibilities for certain activities

- **problem-solving and decision-making** – bringing together skills, talents and responsibilities so that solutions can be applied to particular problems.

The individual's purposes include the means of:

- satisfying social needs through belonging and sharing

- establishing self-concept, enabling people to define themselves in terms of their relationship to others

- gaining help and support to carry out particular objectives

- sharing and helping in a common activity or purpose.

ACTIVITY

1. How many people are in your team?

....

....

2. Is the team based in one or more locations?

....

....

3. Are there teams within teams?

....

....

4. Do some staff work across teams?

....

....

5. Are some staff in teams and also in networks (staff who come together to undertake particular tasks and may come and go depending on the working cycle)?

....

....

Developing teams from groups

It is generally agreed that there are four stages in the development of groups.

● **Forming** – when group members find out about such matters as 'what do others expect of me?', 'how do I behave in this group?' and 'what are the rules in this group?' This is the stage where the individual is trying to establish their personal identity and make their mark on the group.

- **Storming** – when conflict occurs while group members explore roles and relationships in the group. This is the stage where personal agendas are revealed and some inter-personal hostility is present. This is also the stage where the norms of the group are tested.

- **Norming** – when co-operation develops and new 'norms' are developed, including mutual support and the development of a group feeling. This stage is marked by the group establishing how it should work, how it makes decisions and the degree of openness, trust and confidence appropriate to the group.

- **Performing** – when the group is operating effectively as a team, with constructive attempts at task achievement.

It is important to remember that the stages in group development are not necessarily sequential, and that groups can move back and forth between different stages, particularly as group membership changes. When there are significant changes in membership of the group it can experience changes that have been described as **re-forming**.

A group of managers of residential services described the difficulty in supporting the development of a mature team when faced with continual turnover of staff. Collectively they voiced the following view:

> 'We rarely seem to reach a stage of performing. We just get the team established when there's staff movement and the team has to re-form again. You have to constantly remind yourself that you are working with teams that are going through different stages of development and this has implications for how you manage them.'

ACTIVITY

1. Can you identify the stage of development of your team(s)?

....

....

Continued…

ACTIVITY continued

2. What are the implications for the team?

....

....

3. What strategies do you need to develop to enable the team to reach the performing stage?

....

....

....

Interlocking needs of groups

All groups have common needs and these have implications for frontline managers. John Adair has identified them as:

- **task needs** – this is the need to accomplish something. The 'task' is what the group is working on

- **group needs** – the need to develop and maintain the working relationship among group members so that the task can be accomplished. This is concerned with the maintenance needs of the group

- **individual needs** – these are the needs that the individual brings with them into the group, but with membership of the group fulfilling their various needs.

This model, which is also useful when thinking about leadership, provides a helpful way of assessing your team and what needs to take place for the task to be achieved. For example, if the group is motivated then it is more likely to achieve the task. Similarly, if the individual members are motivated then they are likely to work to achieve the task, and also give more to the group.

Defining your team and its responsibilities

Tony Morrison and colleagues from the NSPCC (1987) developed a useful exercise for managers (and team members) that helps in defining the purpose of the team and being clear about your responsibilities. They suggest that managers and teams need to be clear about the specific understanding of the team's mandate as this forms the contract for the work of the team in which both sides (managers and team members) have responsibilities and rights. They stress that it is not something that is passed down from senior managers, but is clarified through ongoing discussion and negotiation between the managers and the team. The importance of this activity is that it can help eliminate misunderstandings, fantasies and covert action about what are the expectations, tasks and resources of the team.

ACTIVITY

Below are listed some of the questions that Morrison and colleagues pose to managers and team members. Jot down your responses to these questions on a separate sheet of paper.

1. What is the mandate for your team – its objectives, responsibilities, powers and areas of discretion?

2. What is the boundary of your team – the limits to its responsibility and individual members' own boundaries, when to say 'yes' and when to say 'no'?

3. Within the boundaries, is there freedom to develop practice in pursuit of team objectives?

4. Does leadership of the team create conditions where people feel good about themselves and produce good results?

The leader and the team

Teams need leaders, but they are not the only ones responsible for how the team runs. Gwen Rosen (1999) reinforces this point, stating that not all tasks have to be led by the team manager – it will be possible to delegate many of these to increase the effectiveness of the work of the team. However, she adds, to maintain credibility within the team the manager should be able to take on most of the team's tasks, even if not to the level of the most experienced members.

Features of the effective team

There are a number of commonly agreed features in teams that are performing effectively.

Task features include:

- having a clear purpose, with all the team members working to an agreed set of objectives
- allocating individuals' roles on the basis of skills, interests and abilities.

Group features include:

- the need to develop and maintain working relationships among members so that the task can be accomplished
- the team meeting together regularly and discussing how they can work effectively together to achieve the agreed objectives
- members listening to each other, building on each other's suggestions and respecting each other's views
- the team having a sense of identity as a separate entity
- the team developing processes for dealing with conflict
- members of the team supporting each other.

Features of the individual team member should include:

- ensuring the individual has space to grow and develop within the team
- ensuring the individual's needs can be met along with, and not at the expense of the group.

eg

In an exercise, residential staff listed some of the factors in effective and ineffective teams in which they had worked:

Effective teams

- good leadership

- clear understanding of the purpose of the team

- the leader briefs the team regularly on changes in the organisation that affect the team

- good working relationships within the team

- enthusiastic team members

- team members have the confidence to express their opinions

- regular team meetings

- regular team-building sessions

- the team has fun!

Ineffective teams

- poor leadership

- unclear aims and objectives

- manager doesn't communicate team issues to senior managers

- lack of support within the team

- team members don't trust each other

- some members are pulling in another direction

- some members have their own agendas which are not discussed in the team

- dominant members

- infrequent meetings

- some members don't feel committed to attending meetings

- information not shared

- important decisions get taken outside the meeting

- constant staff turnover.

Conflict in teams

One area of teamwork mentioned frequently by staff interviewed for this manual was managing conflict, particularly between members of staff teams.

Different views of conflict

Conflict is usually associated with negative features, can be viewed as an expression of feelings and is a form of behaviour that obstructs the achievement of others' goals. On the other hand, it can be seen more constructively as something that can facilitate improvements in services.

Some sources of conflict in teams:

- where there are differences in perception about important issues
- where the work of one member of staff has consequences for another
- where there are values that are deeply held
- where there are individuals narrowly concentrating on particular areas of practice to the neglect of other areas.

Constructive outcomes of conflict include:

- producing new ideas that can lead to solutions to problems
- encouraging team members to seek new approaches
- bringing problems to the surface
- enabling individuals to clarify their views.

Negative outcomes of conflict include:

- mistrust and suspicion developing in the team
- team members becoming defensive
- individual interests taking precedence over team objectives
- people leaving the team
- polarising opinion within the team.

Managing conflict

How you decide to manage conflict will depend on whether you see it as negative or constructive and the extent to which it impacts on the service.

Laurie Mullins (1996) has suggested some strategies that can reduce the negative effects of conflict.

- **Focusing on superordinate goals** that are shared by all members of the team. This can help defuse conflict and lead to more co-operative behaviour. The focus on the shared purpose of the group is described by Charles Handy (1999) as 'drenching the organisation in a common set of values'.

- **Developing interpersonal and group process skills** which can enable team members to better understand their own behaviour, the view-point of others and communication and problem-solving processes.

- **Working on group development activities**, particularly those activities which reduce group cohesion and dysfunctional conflict.

- **Creating a climate of group leadership** which is participative and supportive. This is likely to influence the level of conflict by demonstrating an attitude of respect and trust, encouraging personal development and creating an environment where staff work co-operatively together.

- **Distributing resources equitably** to help overcome conflict about the differences in resources within the group.

Resolving conflict

Where it is not possible to reduce conflict by means of broad strategies then specific steps may need to be taken. Kevin Ford and Sarah Hargreaves (1991) have suggested a process for conflict resolution.

Conflict definition

At this stage it is necessary to define the conflict and reach an agreement on the definition.

1. Describe the disagreement and the differences between individuals.

2. Establish what individuals agree on.

3. Establish what behaviours/actions individuals find acceptable and unacceptable.

4. Establish consensus about possible solutions.

5. Agree what things each individual needs to do to resolve the conflict.

Active listening

Those involved in the conflict need to be sure that they really hear what the others are saying and avoid feelings and opinions obscuring this.

Motivation towards resolution of the conflict

If the attempt at resolution is to be successful, then the people involved should want a resolution. They should examine the gains and losses of continuing the conflict as this may assist in recognising the benefits of resolution and suggest possible solutions.

Reaching an agreement

The agreement should include:

- a statement of the position being adopted

- the ways in which the individuals will act differently in the future

- the ways in which co-operation will be restored if one person acts inappropriately

- the structure and agreed timetable for the parties to meet to discuss their positions and to see if further steps can be taken to improve co-operation.

(Adapted from Ford & Hargreaves, 1991)

Taking action to enhance team performance

Teams that are effective are teams that have an effective leader. As the frontline manager you have the tough job of balancing the sensitivity and support elements of team management with the need to establish clear goals and performance requirements to achieve objectives.

Some of the elements you need to consider to lead your team effectively include:

- promoting the mission of your team. This will act as a motivator

- encouraging openness and involvement of all members in team meetings

- encouraging the team members to support each other, setting the tone by your own supportive behaviour

- encouraging the team to deal with differences of opinion. Being willing to compromise and come to agreement on action with all team members supporting the decisions taken

- reviewing the performance of the team periodically. Identifying what worked well and where improvements are needed, with agreed action taken when performance does not meet agreed standards

- supporting your team in its decision-making functions, based on information gathered, problem recognition, discussion and evaluation of options, before they commit themselves to action

- promoting your the team both within the department and externally, enabling the team's work to be recognised. Make certain that the team's activities integrate with the wider organisation

- celebrating the success of your team through regular feedback, using praise and publicising the success of the team.

Managing yourself as leader of the team

Managing teams can be challenging and difficult work. Many frontline managers reported feeling vulnerable in their position between the demands of senior managers and their team. It is managing this relationship with some of the inevitable tensions that arise that marks out much of the work of the frontline manager. Patricia Kearney (1999) has commented that frontline managers need to engage with rather than avoid the day-to-day problems of their staff.

ACTIVITY

Using the statements on enhancing team performance (see page 96), answer the following questions about the management of your team.

1. Does the team have a clear idea of its purpose?

   ....

   ....

2. Does the team have the opportunity to meet regularly?

   ....

   ....

3. Can the team discuss issues openly and share feelings honestly in meetings?

   ....

   ....

4. How does the team deal with conflict?

   ....

   ....

5. Do you encourage the team to make decisions after proper discussion and ensure that team members agree to support such decisions?

   ....

   ....

6. Does the team have a means of evaluating its performance?

   ....

   ....

7. Do you make certain that you celebrate the success of your team?

   ....

   ....

Teamwork means all team members

Several frontline managers interviewed commented that any discussion of team management should reinforce the point that teams mean everybody in the team, including administrative and support staff. They recognised the tendency for these staff to be ignored, yet they play an important role in enabling other staff to meet the objectives of the service. As frontline manager you need to apply the same principles to administrative and support staff as you would social workers and social care staff. These principles include the following.

- What are the main strengths of the team?

- What are the main weaknesses of the team?

- What are the key issues that the team needs to confront over the next few months if it is to achieve the department's objectives?

KEY POINTS

- ○ Organisations and the individual may have different perceptions of the purpose of teams.

- ○ Teams are continually developing and changes in membership can mean new stages of development with consequences for team effectiveness.

- ○ It is important to define the boundaries of your team and its responsibilities.

- ○ Conflict in teams is common and can express different views about the values and purpose of the team. Its resolution can enable teams to perform more effectively.

- ○ Understanding some of the important elements in managing the team can enhance its performance.

Introduction

As a frontline manager you are in a unique position to develop an under-standing of the changing needs of services users and carers. This means you should be continually thinking about what changes in the service could meet these changing needs. Your approach should be one where you are able to respond rapidly and positively to change opportunities.

Although organisations experience periods of continuity, these are tending to become shorter as services become more sensitive and responsive to their external environment. Organisations are now more likely to reject the notion of ideal organisational structures and systems and to support an approach which values continuous adjustments to systems as part of effective management.

Thinking strategically and developing a responsive service

One of the most important tasks of frontline managers is to generate new ideas and put them into effect as part of developing the organisation's ability to respond to the changing needs of users and carers and demands on the service. A desirable goal is a service that is flexible and responsive and able to adjust to changes in the environment on an incremental basis. This approach means managers anticipate emerging and future needs and organise their resources around them, rather than being unresponsive and ignoring change.

As a frontline manager close to practice you have an important role in initiating change for service improvement. However, you also play an important role in responding to imposed change in the service triggered by the need to respond to new policy initiatives, or by opportunities presented by changes in the external environment of the service.

A key aspect of your role is first, an awareness of the broad thrust of Government policy and how this will impact on practice, and second, understanding the part your management plays in supporting the implementation of policies through change processes. This awareness has a number of features:

- understanding the strategic issues impacting on the organisation and how your team's activities are related to them

- identifying the scope of your team's activities within overall organisational strategies and matching these activities to the external environment in which you operate

- matching activities to the resources available to the team.

ACTIVITY

You will no doubt have experienced many changes in the service when you were a practitioner and have had to implement change.

Reflect on two or three examples of change, writing down your thoughts on a sheet of paper.

1. What were some of the positive features of the change?

2. What were some of the negative aspects of the change?

3. What does this tell you about how the change was introduced and managed?

4. What lessons does it provide you with in approaching the management of change in your team?

Responses to change

In the past, change was seen as an event that interrupted the normal functioning of an organisation. This is now changing as people become more skilled in managing change and more positive about initiating change to improve a service. How staff respond to the opportunities will depend on their disposition to the intended change. Some may be keen on innovation and seek out different ways of doing things; some will be well disposed to change if they see benefits to themselves and the service; others may be resistant, or at least sceptical, until they understand the change more fully and how it will affect them personally.

eg

How staff respond to change will depend on a number of factors which affect them. The following statements were made by managers of residential services who had experience of change management enforced on their service by community care legislation:

- it will mean a change to established ways of working

- will it change social relationships at work?

- it will threaten job security or job prospects

- will it lead to loss of status or self-esteem as a result of enforced changes in role?

- will it mean staff are de-skilled until they learn new methods and achieve new performance standards?

- will it lead to an increase in workload on a temporary or long-term basis?

- will training be provided to help develop the new skills needed?

With so many factors potentially affecting people involved in change it is understandable that some staff may adopt defensive or negative attitudes and resist proposed changes. Your job is to work with staff to enable them to make sense of the need for change, what is required of them and what support they will need.

Good practice in managing change

There are many approaches to the management of change but all tend to converge around a number of essential elements that you need to incorporate into your practice. That said, change is rarely straightforward, and even the best-rehearsed techniques will need to allow for the fact that people react to change in different ways. Change rarely takes a linear path from introduction to implementation. To manage a change process effectively you will need to understand the individual's perspective on change, and the range of responses generated by the introduction of new ways of working.

Your own leadership of the change processes

A major factor in the introduction of change is your own behaviour. A participative style of leadership is helpful as this will allow you to discuss the reasons for change fully with staff and encourage their questions about the change. This will enable them to understand more fully the reasons for change and will also provide valuable feedback for managers on the potential for success. Similarly, involving staff in the implementation process in order to generate commitment and ownership is also crucial.

Trust in your leadership

All large-scale change means stepping into the unknown to some extent and staff will need to trust you as their frontline manager if you are to work effectively in the 'change agent' role. The success of any change will be dependent on a range of often interrelated, complex factors. It is critical that staff trust you to communicate openly with them, to be sensitive to the consequences of your actions and to be prepared to change those actions based on the feedback you receive.

Clarifying what is involved in the change

An important early stage in the management of change is the need to define clearly the purpose of change (the why), what is involved in the change (the what) and the proposed effects of change.

1. **Purpose of change** – what is the objective of change and what are the reasons for it?

2. **What is the nature of the change** – what will be involved in the change?

3. **Effects of change** – the main effects of the change on the organisation and the staff.

Diagnosing receptivity to change

Tom Caple (1990) has described the use of the force field analysis as a diagnostic tool based on the original idea by the social scientist Kurt Lewin. It is a diagrammatic way of mapping the forces which are keeping a particular situation in the current state of equilibrium between the forces pushing for change (the promoting forces) and the forces restraining change (resisting forces).

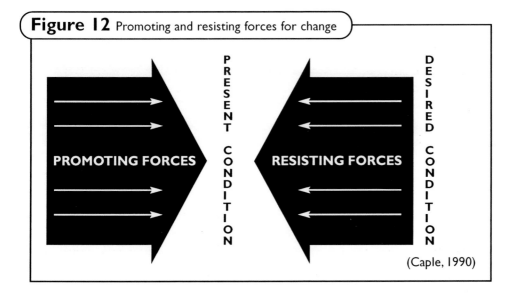

Figure 12 Promoting and resisting forces for change

PROMOTING FORCES

PRESENT CONDITION

RESISTING FORCES

DESIRED CONDITION

(Caple, 1990)

Using the force field analysis

This diagnostic tool will help you:

● provide a picture of the receptivity to change

● identify those factors which will help you implement the change

- identify those factors which will hinder change
- provide a basis for developing the change strategy and methods.

In using the tool you will need to carry out the following steps. Define the problem, stating the current situation and the desired state you wish to achieve, and identifying the forces that are promoting and resisting change.

It is useful to break down the forces under the following headings:

- **personal** – forces inside the individual (or yourself)
- **interpersonal** – forces between individuals (or between you and another person)
- **group** – forces inside the team
- **inter-group** – forces between teams
- **organisational** – forces within the organisation
- **environmental** – forces external to and surrounding the organisation.

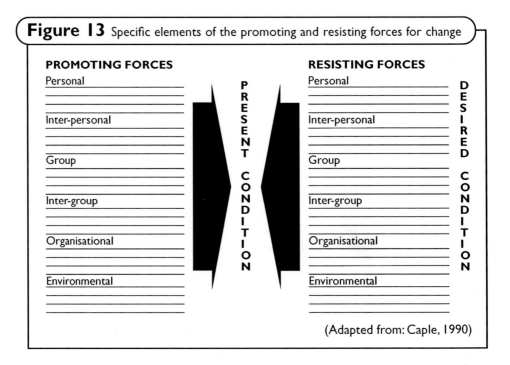

Figure 13 Specific elements of the promoting and resisting forces for change

PROMOTING FORCES

Personal

Inter-personal

Group

Inter-group

Organisational

Environmental

PRESENT CONDITION

RESISTING FORCES

Personal

Inter-personal

Group

Inter-group

Organisational

Environmental

DESIRED CONDITION

(Adapted from: Caple, 1990)

When completing the force field for your service, use arrows of differing lengths to show the relative strength of each force. The longer arrows will indicate stronger forces.

Review the promoting and resisting forces

- Is there a balance or imbalance in the pattern of forces?
- Are any resisting forces being created by promoting forces or vice versa?
- Which are the strongest forces on each side?
- Which resistances could be weakened in their force?
- Which promoting forces could be strengthened?
- Which forces can or cannot be influenced by you?

Resistance to change

Resistance to change can have a number of possible sources, including:

- the reasons for change have not been fully explained
- the current situation is seen as satisfactory and change is not justified
- staff do not feel engaged with the change process
- it will impact on work groups
- it will split up long-standing professional partnerships
- it will affect the shift system or working hours.

ACTIVITY

1. Reflecting on a recent example of change, identify the promoting and resisting forces for change.

....

....

....

Continued…

ACTIVITY continued

2. What actions by the 'change agent' or others altered the relative power of these forces?

....

....

....

3. What does this example tell you about how you could use the force field tool to manage a change situation in the future?

....

....

....

Some ways of working with resistance

● Explain fully why the change is necessary, and what problems it is designed to overcome. Provide staff with a contextual understanding, explaining the internal/external factors which are driving the need for change.

● Encourage staff to participate in the change and engage with the change process. This will provide an opportunity for those likely to be most closely affected by change to suggest ways of improving the planning process.

● Provide staff with the opportunity to voice their objections to the change. This will enable misunderstandings and misconceptions to be discussed and resolved.

Key activities during the change process

● Explain the purpose of the change and why it is necessary. Provide staff with a sense of purpose for the change.

● Communicate a clear sense of direction – expressed ideally as a 'vision'– which staff can relate to the aims of the service.

- Involve those staff affected by change at an early stage and take account of their ideas. Provide opportunities for staff to 'own' the change, although remember you have overall responsibility for the strategic direction of the change.
- Listen to staff and their concerns, acknowledge their fears and work to turn threats into opportunities. Encouraging staff to discuss the change will enable them to feel more committed and also to suggest ways of improving the implementation.
- Identify gaps in skills and arrange developmental opportunities to help staff work in new ways.
- Emphasise the qualitative aspects of change, such as building commitment and trust.
- Recognise that the participative approach to change can be time-consuming and that real progress in change takes time.
- Avoid over-organising.

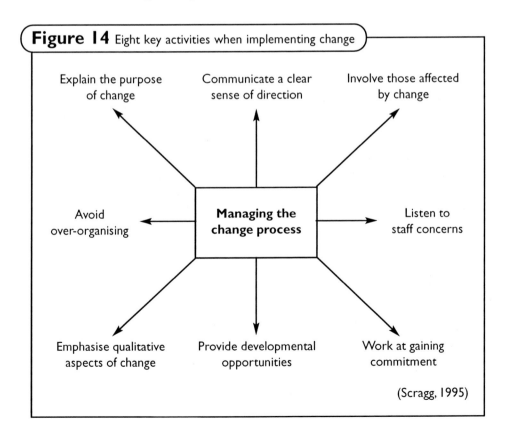

Figure 14 Eight key activities when implementing change

Explain the purpose of change

Communicate a clear sense of direction

Involve those affected by change

Avoid over-organising

Managing the change process

Listen to staff concerns

Emphasise qualitative aspects of change

Provide developmental opportunities

Work at gaining commitment

(Scragg, 1995)

These key activities suggest a number of actions that can improve the introduction and implementation of change. When managing change it is worth making a list of actions that are likely to obstruct change and a list of actions that can reduce obstacles to remind yourself of the issues you are likely to encounter.

Some obstacles to change

- Failing to demonstrate the need for change
- Failing to involve those affected by change in planning and implementation
- Ignoring the norms and social relationships of the group
- Failing to keep staff informed about the change
- Failing to work with staff who will be affected by the change
- Creating excessive demands on staff during implementation.

Ways of reducing obstacles to change

- Involve staff in planning the implementation of change.
- Provide opportunities for staff to question the change and state any concerns or objections.
- Recognise that change can affect the group's norms and social relationships.
- Make only those changes needed and seen as essential.
- Be realistic about the timescale involved to give staff time to adapt to new ways of working.
- Ensure staff have access to training when new skills are needed.
- Ensure that staff have the resources needed to carry out the new ways of working.

(Adapted from Ford & Hargreaves, 1990)

(KEY POINTS)

○ Recognise the human and social factors involved in change.

○ Understand that resistance to change provides an opportunity to work with staff and understand their fears and concerns.

○ Recognise that the change can have unintended consequences for staff and the service.

○ Remember that managing change is related to many other areas of management, including leadership, motivation, teamwork and managing performance.

Managing partnerships

Introduction

Frontline managers in social care services have traditionally worked across organisational boundaries as part of the complex web of agencies delivering services. What has now changed is the emphasis in the Government's modernisation agenda on the idea of 'partnership' and its corollary of 'joined up' working. Partnerships are concerned with the interface of social care and healthcare, but also with users and carers and a wide range of services provided at local and central government levels.

eg

An indication of the importance of partnership working can be judged from the survey conducted by Sue Balloch and colleagues in the mid-90s which found that two-thirds of managers and three-quarters of social workers included joint working with other agencies in their main responsibilities. With the introduction of the modernisation agenda this has now become an even more important area of responsibility.

(Balloch *et al,* 1999)

Partnerships with other agencies

The underlying theme in all the policy documents (for example, the NHS and Social Services White Papers, the NHS Plan and National Service Frameworks), is the development of a culture of and commitment to supporting partnership working between social care services and health services (and other services such as education and housing). Moreover, there is now a requirement that all services commit themselves to working across organisational boundaries, in order to create a more integrated service delivery framework. The main mechanisms to achieve these policy objectives are pooled budgets, lead commissioning, and integrated provision all of which have begun to develop under new powers contained in the *Health Act 1999*.

Health Act 1999 'flexibilities'

The *Health Act 1999* is a new piece of legislation in relation to partnership working that has introduced three new 'flexibilities' which have considerable significance for social care agencies. These flexibilities include the potential to create partnership working through the following mechanisms:

- pooled budgets across health and local authority services

- lead commissioning, allowing the delegation of functions: for example, a health authority, primary care trust or social services department to become the lead commissioner for a particular service

- integrated provision: for example, allowing the delegation of functions such as a NHS mental health trust to deliver both health and social care services.

eg

The Audit Commission (2000) had identified a number of examples of joint working in services for older people where multidisciplinary teams made up of health and social care staff work to a single line manager who holds a pooled budget, with the manager reporting to a board made up of representatives of the different agencies funding the service, for example, health authorities and local authorities.

Levels of partnership working

TOPSS (1999) has identified a number of levels of partnership working between social care and health services – these include strategic, operational and service delivery levels.

- **Strategic level**. Mechanisms such as joint planning and lead commissioning. Examples include social services departments, health authorities and primary care groups giving the lead commissioning role to a social services department to provide services for older people.

- **Operational level**. Multidisciplinary teams and interdisciplinary groupings based in the same location: for example, community mental health and learning disabilities teams and new teams emerging from the *Health Act 1999* provisions.

- **Service delivery level**. Case-by-case collaboration between frontline staff (including frontline managers), collaborating with others based in separate locations. It is recognised that a large number of the social care workforce will be involved in joint or collaborative working at this level.

Working in partnership with other agencies: issues for the frontline manager

The requirement to work in partnership with other agencies means that frontline managers will increasingly need to collaborate with other agencies, and may find themselves in single line manager roles in the future, where they are responsible for staff from other agencies. This will mean learning about the different values bases, goals and objectives of other agencies which will influence the effectiveness of partnership working. The NHS, voluntary and private agencies, for example, have different values, cultures, structures and working processes that have been formed over many years. Working more closely with them means understanding the differences and recognising the consequences of these differences so that the goal of delivering more effective services is not undermined.

> 'The Government's agenda is crystal clear – you will work together by pooling resources to provide benefits for the user – but it's not easy for managers. You've got to recognise the different cultures, who holds power and how decisions get made. The value base can be quite different and it takes time to get used to the language, the acronyms and just the different way services are provided.'
>
> **Service manager**

Staff development implications

Working in partnership has implications for the development of staff and how they see their role. Increasingly staff will need to:

- understand the reasons for partnership working

- recognise working across agency boundaries as the norm

- learn about other agencies and their ways of working in order to be effective in their role as representatives of their own organisation

- work in partnership with other professionals while retaining clear social care objectives.

These are all areas of practice where you can support your staff through supervision, training and development opportunities that enable the service to meet the requirements for effective partnerships.

> 'Although it was time consuming and difficult at first, I think it's been useful to have been on the PCG (primary care group). I feel I have been able to make a contribution and represent the views of social services in the group. The work we have done in the department with users' and carers' consultation shows that we are ahead of the game in some ways.'
>
> **Service manager**

Relevant learning from earlier work on community care development

Some of the early work undertaken by the National Health Service Training Directorate and the Social Services Inspectorate (1993) as part of the community care changes still holds good for the new work on partnerships. This work was concerned with enabling managers to work across the boundaries of health, social services and the voluntary sector and enable them to manage services effectively in partnership. Some of the key issues to emerge from this work are listed overleaf.

- Working in partnership means working with agencies that have different goals and objectives, and understanding the basis for these differences.

- It is important to recognise that different organisations have their own goals, objectives and priorities and that these can lead to communication problems between organisations and their staff.

- Work on identifying goals and expectations of working in partnership was helpful to participants.

- Exercises to recognise and understand stereotypes were helpful.

- Exchanging information about each others' services was helpful.

- Exploring new areas of practice was helpful for staff.

- Seeing the world through others' eyes widens understanding of other services.

The more this development work can be undertaken jointly with colleagues from other services, the more effective partnership working will become. Inter-agency learning opportunities can lead to the development of a broader understanding and new skills and attitudes which are quite different from those learned from work within a single organisation.

eg

Work by TOPSS (1999) on identifying the training needs of staff in social services found that frontline staff are increasingly involved in joint or collaborative working and identified priorities for staff development. These include, staff in multidisciplinary teams needing knowledge and skills in working with personnel from other agencies as well as with other disciplines in their own multidisciplinary teams.

Working in partnership with users and carers

More effective partnerships with users and carers is another example of aspects of the Government modernisation agenda which require commissioners and providers of services to develop partnerships in order to make services more responsive to users' and carers' needs. It is intended that these priorities be achieved through a range of initiatives, including:

- providing better information about available services to potential users – the 'one stop shop'
- providing services which are more responsive both in speed and convenience of delivery
- improving assessment and review procedures
- tailoring services more to the needs and lifestyles of users
- consulting users and using their views to shape future services provision
- ensuring stronger safeguards for users through new developments in inspection and complaints procedures.

eg

A King's Fund report on community care identifies what users want from services:

- responsive and flexible so they fit in with people's individual circumstances
- of good quality with staff having the appropriate skills
- work carried out in the home should be of a good standard
- services should be integrated, with staff dealing with boundary problems, rather than users.

(King's Fund, 1999)

Working in partnership with users and carers: implications for the frontline manager

First and foremost you must recognise the changing relationships between the service and users and carers, where access to information is a right and there are clear expectations about what services can be provided.

However, focusing on the following specific areas will help you manage this change in 'culture':

- recognising the users and carers will be more empowered, with access to information and the ability to challenge professionals' decisions

- using feedback from users and carers when evaluating different interventions techniques in order to understand what works

- drawing on evidence-based research (see **Appendix 1** for websites) to confirm existing practice or support new approaches to service delivery

- using management information systems to develop a knowledge base in order to make judgements about levels of need, service outcomes and continuous improvement.

'The frontline manager is a key person who can influence the department's strategy if they are working to develop consumer involvement in service delivery and can feed consumer issues to senior management. We rely on the front line for this information.'

Social services manager

Supporting staff working in partnership with users and carers

The development of a more consumerist approach in services has consequences for staff. A number of managers interviewed described the demands new ways of working with users and carers were having on their staff, particularly where staff found themselves in more challenging relationships. They found that personal accountability had increased, and users and carers questioned their decisions more frequently, including resorting to the use of complaints procedures if dissatisfied with the service's responses.

TOPSS (1999) has identified four goals in its training strategy for partnership working:

- agencies and staff should be committed to work in partnership with one another and with users and carers

- staff of different disciplines should have the knowledge, skills and values necessary to work collaboratively on joint decisions

- organisational and service-funding frameworks should support and facilitate partnership working and attitudes

- levels of partnership skills and the effectiveness of related training and development should be monitored, and examples of good practice disseminated.

KEY POINTS

○ With changes in Government policy and new legislation the growth of partnership working between social care agencies and other services is increasingly rapidly.

○ New forms of partnership working are already in place and are likely to develop rapidly as a result of pressure from Government and more flexibility in the budgeting and management of services.

○ Working in partnership with other agencies means understanding the differences in values and cultures as well as priorities and objectives and how these differences can affect partnership strategies.

○ The growing expectation that users and carers should be consulted and involved in services needs to be acknowledged, with its consequences for changes in the relationship with professionals.

○ Partnerships with other agencies and with users and carers have significant training implications for staff at all levels in services. Earlier work by the NHS Service Training Directorate and the Social Services inspectorate has identified some of the key issues.

Introduction

Responsibility for financial management is increasingly being devolved to frontline managers. The intention is to devolve greater power and control to managers and thereby allow for more sensitive tailoring of the service and greater innovation. The intention of passing on control of budgets to frontline managers is to help them make more effective decisions and manage budgets better. The advantages are that you have a degree of control over the budget management process and are able to allocate resources to areas that require support based on frontline information.

There are a number of reasons for the devolvement of financial management to frontline managers. These include:

- providing incentives for a cost-effective use of resources
- enabling frontline managers to make better decisions on priorities
- linking managerial and financial responsibility at the point where resources are deployed
- facilitating flexible responses to the needs of users and carers
- helping to speed up decision-making
- increasing accountability.

'Since I've been responsible for my budget I've been able to alter the staffing to meet pressures on the home. I've reduced a management post to be able to employ more care staff as the dependency levels of residents has increased. I didn't have that flexibility before.'

Residential manager

Cost centres

Part of the evolving process of change in local authority and independent sector financial management has been the establishment of cost centres, where definable areas of activity (eg a social work team) are identified. In addition, the manager (team manager) is given responsibility for the delivery of a particular set of services, the costs of which are quantified, managed and related to the services provided to users and carers. This process ideally enables the manager to see the relationship between the way resources are deployed and the expenditure under their control.

What budget management means for the frontline manager

Your main task is to monitor spending against the amounts approved and this is normally carried out through a regular monthly report which states expenditure being incurred against the budget. You are a 'budget holder' and given authority to spend money in order to achieve targets in relation to the overall plan for the department. You are responsible for achieving the budget and ensuring that funds are available for making a commitment on expenditure. Information for monitoring and decision-making purposes is increasingly provided online, enabling you to receive prompt information on expenditure as agencies extend their computer networks to local offices and residential and day service facilities.

eg

A budget holder's charter

The Scottish Borders Social Work Department has developed a budget holder's charter with the following definition of the budget holder:

> 'A budget holder is a person responsible for controlling expenditure and/or income against one or more budget headings.'

The charter states that budget holders have a series of specific responsibilities:

- to acquaint themselves with the council's financial regulations
- to consider the availability of the budget before authorising expenditure

Continued…

eg continued

- to report significant variances to their line manager
- to initiate the correction of any miscoding which appears against their budgets
- to contribute to the budget preparation process
- to familiarise themselves with the assumptions that underlie their final approved budget.

To undertake the responsibilities involved with managing a budget, managers have a number of rights, including:

- access to appropriate training
- reliable information
- access to advice and support when needed
- to contribute to the initial preparation of the budget
- that any virements will be requested by them or will come to them for agreement before formal approval is sought.

(Page & Gilder, 2000)

Some problems with devolved budgeting

In spite of the increased shift to devolved budget management at the front line, this process can be undermined by a number of factors. Richard Field (1999) has listed some of the problems that can affect the commitment of frontline managers to endorse budget management:

- budget preparation and control is separated from service planning and management
- budget managers have little scope to manage, and in effect can only administer their budgets
- managers feel unable to shape their budgets, and as a consequence lack commitment to achieving a budget they have had no hand in preparing
- start–stop spending during the year, culminating in 'spend it or lose it'

- unnecessary involvement of the finance department staff in budget management.

Field sees five main reasons for this situation:

- the organisation fails to recognise that devolving budgets means a shift in power, increased discretion at the front line and reduced detailed central control

- budgets continue to be prepared by someone else and are subject to 'cuts' which the manager is expected to absorb

- the financial systems are based on those designed for accountants and managers find the presentation of information unhelpful

- continued use of incremental budgeting, often with the application of *pro rata* cuts even though there are greater demands on the service which must be achieved with less resources.

ACTIVITY

1. Do you have an opportunity to prepare and negotiate your budget?

....

....

2. Have you received training in financial management?

....

....

3. Do the financial and management information systems support your budget management responsibilities?

....

....

Continued…

ACTIVITY continued

4. Do you know the details of your budget before the year begins and the level of service it is expected to support?

....

....

5. Is the year-end service and budget performance reviewed in order to apply any lessons to future years?

....

....

(Adapted from: Field, 1999)

Budgeting: key stages

The budget cycle

The budget cycle in social services departments begins in the autumn each year as senior managers consider the needs of the department in relation to new policies and existing commitments. By November local authorities will have been informed by the Government about their revenue support grant for the coming year, and by January will have agreed their service budgets.

The budget process

A budget is essentially a plan for the coming year that is expressed in financial terms. There are several stages to developing this plan, and ideally you should be involved in all of them. In preparing the budget an organisation will examine its activities for the year, which are then translated into the financial resources needed to implement them. The traditional way in which resources are allocated in social services departments is by a process called 'incremental budgeting'. The current year's budget is the base budget and it is updated (incremented) for inflation and other commitments. The main determinants are this year's and past years' allocations.

The important questions that this form of budget planning raises are whether items are still required and the amounts allocated appropriately. The alternative is zero-based budgeting where every item is assessed for the first time. Incremental budgeting is nevertheless widely used because so many items and activities are for statutory services or are so fundamental to the organisation that they will continue each year. What is important is that the activities are continually reviewed and zero-based methods used where appropriate.

Planning the budget

This is an important part of the budget holder's responsibility. Participating in the budget-planning stage will enable you to consider how the service is performing and how conditions may change in the next year and to determine the financial implications of these changes. You may also have identified areas of the service you wish to change if the budget allows.

If you are responsible for the budget then you should be involved in the process of preparing it. This will allow you to participate in the process, provide greater ownership and increase your commitment to managing your budget effectively and to meeting agreed targets. Your job is to assess the needs and resources required to achieve particular levels of service and submit these in budgetary terms to your manager for approval.

Although this is the ideal situation, the reality is that many social services departments are unsure of the money available until close to the beginning of the financial year, so the extent of your participation in budget-planning for your service may be limited.

Setting the budget

In setting the budget a number of factors will be taken into account:

- is the current budget sufficient for the coming year's activity?
- is it logical, does it meet the requirements of the different aspects of your teamwork?
- are there known or likely service changes next year?
- are there service priorities which you have to take into account?

ACTIVITY

To clarify your financial responsibility, answer the following questions.

1. What areas of expenditure have been devolved to you?

   ....

   ....

2. What areas of expenditure are retained centrally?

   ....

   ....

3. On what basis was the budget allocation made to you as a devolved budget holder?

   ....

   ....

4. What powers of virement have you been given?

   ....

   ....

5. Are there penalties incurred for overspending?

   ....

   ....

Monitoring your budget

Once your budget is allocated you will need to monitor it. Each month you will receive from the finance department a statement of your expenditure to date, either as a computer print-out or on your computer screen. This statement is the finance department's view of your expenditure (and income, depending on the service) during the defined budget period. It compares the finance department's view of what you should have spent (and earned, depending on the service) with your agreed budget.

This statement will enable the results of the month's expenditure to be compared to the budget, and the predicted effects on the end of year position. This statement provides you with information about the expenditure you control and enables you to compare it with your budget. Your main responsibility is to note any differences against the profile, any likely variations and where virement is needed. The main area for your attention will be the overspends and underspends, which are known as variances.

What the budget information looks like

When the budget is issued to you it will be split up into lines. Each line will be your authorisation to spend up to an agreed limit on certain items. The budget may also have columns, probably on a monthly basis, which split your authorisation up into time periods and reflect the anticipated profile of expenditure for your service throughout the year.

The lines will usually be divided into pay and non-pay items, with the pay items usually the greater part. Pay items will be related to your staffing establishment so that you know how many staff you should have, their salary grades, wages and any overtime that you may authorise, and how many agency hours can be purchased. The statement will also contain information on vacancies and when they can be filled.

Non-pay items are usually a considerably smaller element of your monthly budget statement, and refer to items such as furniture, domestic supplies and equipment.

eg

Example of a budget statement

Although budget statements vary to some extent in different agencies, each will have a core of infomation which is broadly similar, including lines (horizontal) and columns (vertical). A typical budget statement which arrives on your desk or computer screen each month is a statement of what has happened in the preceding budget period. The following example is based on a residential home and has excluded for simplicity a number of lines for separate items of expenditure and the cumulative columns.

Items	Annual budget	Monthly budget	Expenditure	Variance
This column will list the budget heads for the cost centre	Annual budgetary authorisation for the cost centre	Monthly budgetary authorisation	Actual month's expenditure	Identifies the variances (overspends and under-spends) in the preceding budget period
Staff This will usually have separate lines for: ● salaried staff ● weekly paid staff ● agency staff.				
Supplies This will include items such as: ● food ● medicines ● laundry.				
Services This will include items such as: ● maintenance ● equipment ● vehicle fuel.				

Virement

If your budget shows a mix of overspends and underspends and these variances are not caused by inaccurate profiling of your budget (how the expenditure will occur on a month-by-month basis) then you should have the possibility of viring expenditure from one head to another. Virement is the ability to transfer money from one (underspent) budget to another (sometimes overspent) one. It is likely that your department will have rules which state what virement is allowed within the budget and who needs to agree action. For a more detailed examination of budgetary control, Bernard Jones's (1997) book on public sector finance provides a clear and concise explanation of the manager's responsibilities (see recommended reading in **Appendix 1** on which I have drawn extensively for this section of the chapter).

ACTIVITY

Are you clear about the budget information you receive?

1. Is the summary accurate?

....

2. Is it giving you the correct information?

....

3. Is the information outdated?

....

4. Are you clear about the costs you can control and those you cannot?

....

'Keeping within budget'

The budget statement is the means by which the organisation communicates information to you about the activity levels and financial consequences of the previous month's activity. Your responsibility as the budget holder will be to 'keep within your budget', although you need to be clear about what your responsibilities are and how much control you have over the budget. For example, you may have only limited control over spending. It may be the case that:

- you only have the use of a single residential home which leaves you with no scope for getting a better deal
- staffing levels and salary costs of your team are fixed
- costs on your budget for central services are outside your control.

Responsibility for the budget

What you need to clarify is the extent of your responsibility as a budget holder and what freedom you have to vire between budget heads and to control spending in terms of staffing (usually your major expenditure), and the purchase of suppliers and services. Questions to ask include:

- what is the extent of your power in relation to your budget?
- are you held responsible for overspends?
- what are the limits of your authority for expenditure?

Accountability

You also need to clarity your accountability in relation to your budget responsibilities. How frequently are you expected to report to your line manager?

Scope of your budgetary power

Your budget will provide information on expenditure in two areas:

- revenue expenditure – expenditure on day-to-day running costs such as salaries, stationery etc
- capital expenditure – expenditure on things of lasting value such as buildings, major items of equipment etc.

Power to make budgetary decisions

Your main power will be in relation to revenue expenditure, particularly staffing where you will need to make decisions within your budget responsibility about the staffing level of your service. You are also likely to have some limited power over minor capital expenditure – often for relatively small items such as furniture and equipment – which will include the purchase of goods and services from outside the organisation.

Social services activities are labour intensive, with a large percentage of total costs being wages and salaries. Staff are also on nationally agreed pay scales which reduces your flexibility to control your budget. Your freedom in budgetary terms will mainly be through the limited virement between certain budget heads. Virement is the principle of moving funds from one budget head to another and is a major tool in terms of flexibility. It can be the key to your control over resources. You need to be clear about the limits of your power to vire between budget heads so that you are confident about the decisions you are making.

Turning financial information into management information

The line budgets provide you with information on the staffing and equipment you need to ensure that the service is being delivered effectively. In monitoring the expenditure the budget will show you whether you have over or under spent on particular budget heads. This information can then be translated from quantitative information to management information to enable you to understand how the service is being provided and the consequences of financial decisions on your service.

Variances

Comparing the actual revenues and expenditures with the budget will usually show up differences, known as 'variances'. Variances are common and to be expected and have a number of causes, including:

- a planning variance where an assumption about staffing costs has not been met because the post has not been filled. This is likely to be outside your control

- a volume variance may arise where the number of service users has increased over a period and is greater than was predicted. Again it may not be possible to control this factor if demands on the service are higher than anticipated

- price variance is where the cost of supplies is higher than expected. Your control here is to try to achieve better terms from suppliers, although this will depend on the local authority's policies on suppliers

- efficiency variances are related to the level of resources used. For example, a residential home needed greater agency cover because of staff sickness. Again you may have little control over this additional expenditure if it is caused by unforeseen circumstances. Management action to keep within your budget for agency cover means addressing issues that result in surges in agency costs.

The important issue is to identify the reasons for the variances and to what extent you can control them and, importantly, whether they are within your control. Whichever reason is found they should inform you about strategies for managing your budget and reducing discrepancies and planning for the future.

The role of an agency's accountants

It is important to remember that devolved responsibility does not mean you are on your own! Finance staff are there to provide support and training as well as regular information. Their job is to support you and provide budget management advice and training. It is important to use these services, particularly if you have not managed a budget before.

'We've devolved budgets to individual budget holders and they are in control now with power to decide what to do with their budget. The decision-making is easier for them when the resources are under their control. The budget information is to enable them to do their job, but we're here to back them up. If they're worried we are on the end of the phone. I see us as part of the team supporting the frontline managers.'

Finance manager

What you should expect from the financial support team

- Someone to answer your questions when and where you need them.

- The provision of a level of good quality information which means that you will need to ask elementary questions less frequently as time goes on.

- The encouragement of a 'learning culture' where you can feel comfortable questioning financial support staff on any aspect of budget management.

KEY POINTS

○ As frontline managers you will be expected to take responsibility for the budget for your team or unit.

○ Request training in budget management if this is a new area of responsibility for you.

○ You should be involved in the budget process from the beginning. In this way you will be able to contribute to decisions about the allocation of financial resources for your part of the service.

○ You will need to become familiar with interpreting the financial statements you receive each month.

○ If you are concerned about the content of the statement discuss this with your line manager or the finance department.

○ Responsibility for your budget means that you should have some flexibility to make decisions that improve the service.

○ You are not expected to have the skills of an accountant and should draw on the expertise of the finance support team.

Managing information

Introduction

The management of information is a relatively recent area of study for managers but one that is becoming increasingly important, particularly with advances in technology which have made it possible to store great volumes of data and retrieve them quickly for decision-making purposes. Large amounts of data from outside the organisation can also be accessed rapidly through the use of the internet and can increase our understanding of policy initiatives and practice issues influenced by research findings. A further development is the increasing use of websites by local authorities and other organisations which can be accessed by users and carers to increase their understanding of services available.

Information management at the front line

Your location at the front line of the service means that you have an important role in the management of information. You will receive information from frontline staff and others that will assist you in managing staff workloads, measuring performance and evaluating the outcomes of interventions. Some of this information will need to be passed on to your line manager for use collectively to review the effectiveness of services and to plan for the future.

> 'One of the biggest potential problems is the gulf between senior management and practice. As a team manager I see my job as making the connection between these two worlds, with communication vital in bridging this gulf.'
>
> Team manager

Similarly, you will also receive information from senior managers and your line manager about changes and adjustments needed in the management of the service in the light of strategic and policy changes, resource changes and other initiatives, which you need to communicate to your team. This is a vital part of managing information if staff at the front line are to be kept fully informed about departmental decisions. You can increase your effectiveness in this area by discussing with the team what information needs they have and how you can best communicate with them.

Your crucial information management role

A crucial part of the frontline management role is the potential to transmit information in the organisation. Gwen Rosen (2000) has likened a social service department to an hourglass with the frontline manager situated at the narrowest part. Situated here you are located on the border between senior management and frontline staff. Through you information is passed down by senior managers and on (or not) to staff. Similarly, you are the channel through which information is passed upwards (or not) to senior managers.

Rosen argues that you need to have a detailed understanding of what your staff are doing and be able to communicate this information to others. If this is not done senior management will not receive feedback from the front line and management can become detached from practice, with little control over the performance of the organisation.

Information flows and management levels

The Social Services Inspectorate (1997), in their review of information strategies and systems, has described the information flow and management levels in a social services department. This identifies the operational management level (approximating to the front line) as an area where a considerable range of information concerning service user needs, services requested and service provided is important in planning the delivery of services.

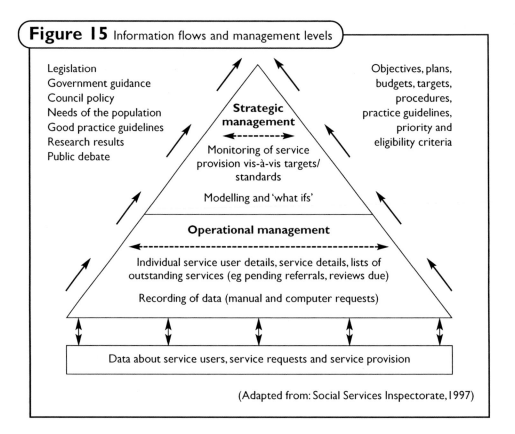

Figure 15 Information flows and management levels

Legislation
Government guidance
Council policy
Needs of the population
Good practice guidelines
Research results
Public debate

Strategic management

Monitoring of service provision vis-à-vis targets/ standards

Modelling and 'what ifs'

Operational management

Individual service user details, service details, lists of outstanding services (eg pending referrals, reviews due)

Recording of data (manual and computer requests)

Objectives, plans, budgets, targets, procedures, practice guidelines, priority and eligibility criteria

Data about service users, service requests and service provision

(Adapted from: Social Services Inspectorate, 1997)

ACTIVITY

Using the diagram above, think about the following areas. You might like to note down your ideas on a blank sheet of paper.

- Using the diagram, identify the types of information that are collected, where the information comes from, what you do with it and where it needs to be passed on to.

- How effective is the information flow in meeting the needs of the organisation, both at the front line and through the different levels of management?

Table 2 Information requirements and the demands made on the frontline manager

Concerns of each group which place information demands on the frontline manager	The information required
General public What services are provided? Where the public can access information?	Information on service provision Contact points for services
Service users and carers What care options are available? Who can provide this care? What are the costs of this care? What can I do if I don't get what I want?	How different care options can be met Service costings Services users' rights, and complaints procedures
Staff team What are the team/departmental objectives? Who will do what, when? What resources are available? What are the service standards to be used? What training is available?	Team/departmental objectives Team workload plan Team resource plan Team quality standards Training and development plan
Senior managers What is the performance of your service? What is it achieving? What is it costing? What are its likely future needs?	Activity statistics Outcome measures Expenditure statements Forecasts of future demands
Service commissioners What are the needs of the local population? What is the current pattern of care services? What activity is contracted with the independent sector? What are the costs of providing services? What are the problems concerned with providing contracted services?	Forecasts of service demand Present activity information Contracted activity Expenditure on contracted services Resourcing or quality problems
Other teams/departments/agencies What demands will other agencies place on you? What services can other agencies provide to you? What are the costs involved?	Demands to provide services for your team or unit Requirements for services from other services Data on service costs
Suppliers What demands will you place on suppliers? What services can the supplier provide to you? What are the costs involved?	Demands to provide services to you Requirements for services from you Cost data from suppliers

(Adapted from: Shanahan, 1999)

ACTIVITY

- What does this table suggest in terms of the information different groups require from you?

- Where are the difficulties in accessing information to meet their needs?

Information needs of different groups

A helpful way of making sense of the management of information is to identify the requirements different groups have for information and what demands this makes on you.

Discussion with managers and practitioners highlighted the problems around information management, particularly in terms of data collection. Many frontline staff saw data inputting as taking them away from 'more important practice', whereas managers recognised that without up-to-date and high quality data it was not possible to plan services that reflected the needs of local populations. Jean Jeffrey (1996) discusses the dilemmas that affect different staff groups.

The role of frontline staff in data collection

Frontline staff are in a key position to collect of much of the data needed by social services departments for decision-making purposes. Jeffrey argues that they will not be motivated to carry this out, or at least not with care, if they cannot see the benefits to be gained for their efforts, particularly where this competes with other practice demands.

For this activity to succeed she suggests that practitioners will want to see immediate and simple access to:

- client information and previous service use
- assessment and care plan details
- availability/price/quality of service
- care management budgets.

This information is important in supporting the work of frontline staff who are:

- conducting assessments, agreeing care plans and ordering services
- calculating costs of care packages and charges to clients
- recording outcomes and reviews.

Enabling staff who are under pressure to see the importance of this information is a vital part of the frontline management role.

The frontline manager's role in supporting data collection

You have an important role here in supporting staff who are the main information source about user and carer needs, and in ascertaining which interventions work and which do not. Barbara Hearn and colleagues (1992) have argued that information broadens a team's vision of practice and the issues with which they must grapple. Without current and relevant information and actions, decisions are likely to be based as much on assumption and prejudice as on knowledge. An important task for the frontline manager is to evaluate the information collected and assess its usefulness, ensuring that it is commensurate with the effort required to gather it.

The use of collected data by senior managers

According to Jean Jeffrey (1996), senior managers have different information needs, and rely on data collected by frontline staff. Collected data play an important role in informing managers who need to make decisions based on such information, including:

- local demographic changes
- incidence of need
- financial monitoring
- assessment information
- service use patterns
- contract monitoring.

This data will support:

- population needs and forecasting
- strategic planning
- market mapping
- budget control
- joint commissioning
- performance management
- statutory returns.

What are your information management needs?

It is traditionally assumed that most management decisions are based on hard information: for example, statistical reports, budgetary monitoring statements etc. In reality it is likely that most decisions are based on soft information: for example, meetings with team colleagues, conversations with other managers and telephone calls.

It is also important to acknowledge that the greatest volume of information relevant to your frontline management role is informal, qualitative and verbal. Your day-to-day management responsibilities mean you need information that is up-to-date because of the urgency of much of your decision-making.

There are many reasons for this, including the opportunity soft information provides for you to access the sources of this information to gain precise answers. First, it is useful to identify your information needs in relation to your role as a frontline manager. Second, identify your main responsibilities and what these mean in terms of the information that you need for decision-making purposes. Where can you find this information and how you can use it?

ACTIVITY

1. Give some examples of hard and soft information that you have received recently.

. . . .

. . . .

. . . .

2. What use did you make of the different sorts of information?

. . . .

. . . .

. . . .

Continued…

ACTIVITY continued

3. Was it helpful for decision-making purposes?

....

....

....

4. What were the strengths and weaknesses of the hard and soft information you identified?

....

....

....

Evaluating hard information

When you receive hard information it is helpful to assess its quality by using the following criteria to judge its value to you.

- Was it **accurate**?
- Was it **adequate** to enable you to interpret the data and use it as a basis for action?
- Was it **relevant**?
- Was it **timely** and available when you needed it?
- Was the **quantity** adequate, not too much and not too little?
- Was it **reliable and trustworthy**?
- Was it **suitable** for your purposes and in a user-friendly form?
- Was it **presented in a style that was accessible**?
  (Adapted from: Open College, 1992)

ACTIVITY

Think about the various forms of hard information you receive: for example, financial statements, annual reports, information on referrals etc. Using the above list of characteristics, assess your objectives for the various pieces of information you receive.

1. Are they meeting your information needs?

2. What does this now tell you about the information that you communicate to others?

3. Would it be helpful to think about these factors when you are preparing documents for others?

Meetings

Because managers report spending a considerable amount of their time in meetings with team members and other managers, it is important to consider the effectiveness of this activity in terms of their information exchange role. From the comments of managers consulted for this manual, meetings can be a major source of frustration, with many displaying the following weaknesses:

- called for reasons that are not clear
- no agenda, or agenda given out at the meeting with no time to consider whether the manager needs to be present
- ineffective chairing
- diverted by vocal members with their own agendas
- resulting in no clear decisions being taken.

ACTIVITY

Veronica Coulshed (1990) describes some of the heavy resource costs of meetings and lists some essential points to consider about meetings. Think of a recent meeting you attended and answer the following questions on a separate sheet of paper.

1. Was the meeting really necessary or could the matters be resolved by other means of communication (eg letters or memos, email, individual meetings with staff)?

Continued…

ACTIVITY continued

2. Did the agenda indicate the function of each item (eg 'for discussion', 'for decision', 'for information')?

3. Was the agenda circulated in advance but not so far in advance that people mislaid it?

4. Were start and finish times stated?

5. Did the meeting start on time?

6. Did the chair state what the meeting was intended to achieve?

7. Did people who hogged the discussion get a clear signal from the chair that it was 'time to move on'?

8. Did the agenda avoid 'any other business' (often a time waster and used to introduce complex issues needing more time)

9. Did the agenda start with the controversial items and end with items that unite the group?

10. Did the chair summarise the results of the discussion at the end of each item to assist minute-taking and to confirm what had been achieved?

11. Did the number of people attending create a workable size for the intended purpose? (Coulshed suggests that about 12 people is the maximum if everyone is to participate.)

Points to consider when you are next invited to a meeting or are planning a meeting

- Should we be having a meeting or can decisions be taken without bringing people together?
- Is the purpose of the meeting clear?
- Who should be invited to attend?
- When and where will the meeting be held?

More effective meetings

Patricia Kearney (1999) sees the frontline manager as having the potential to create an effective and dynamic team environment through the way

they manage meetings and their expectations about team colleagues'
performance in relation to meetings. For example:

- Is there an expectation that all staff will attend meetings on time?

- Is there an expectation that all staff will attend meetings unless there
  is an appropriate reason for absence?

- Is there an expectation that staff will come to meetings with the
  necessary documents?

Facilitation of meetings

Kearney suggests that the effectiveness of teamwork is enhanced by the
way in which meetings are facilitated by the frontline manager. This can
be done by ensuring that the following takes place:

- there is clear communication throughout the meeting

- differences of opinion are acknowledged and openly discussed

- an environment is created where staff are confident enough to
  present their views and know they will be listened to

- the focus of the meeting is bounded by professional discussion
  and is on the direct work of the team and not submerged beneath
  organisational business or generalities not connected to the focus of
  the topic under discussion

- the frontline manager feels confident to make decisions in the meeting
  and state clearly why decisions have been taken

- there is an expectation that the team will agree on action to be taken

- there is clarity about the team's tasks and the limits and purpose of
  the team

- there is respect for other people's skills, experience and specialist
  knowledge within the team.

Meetings with other managers

Another important part of your role will be meeting with other managers,
both from within your organisation and from other agencies. It is useful
to assess your own performance as a participant and decide whether you
feel you achieved your objectives.

ACTIVITY

● Did I prepare for the meeting?

....

● Did I contribute too little or too much?

....

● Did I listen to the views of other participants?

....

● Did I influence the meeting positively or negatively?

....

The role of information technology

As a manager you need to develop an understanding of information management and its benefits and drawbacks, particularly with respect to information technology. This knowledge and these skills are becoming greater as social care agencies become more complex, with greater financial accountability, and increased monitoring and regulation, which all require skills and understanding in terms of management responsibilities.

It is also increasingly important because of the role information now plays in organisations as part of the wider changes in the management of services.

The importance of information management is becoming increasingly urgent as social care agencies shift from traditional paper-based systems to computer-based systems. This is because although the growth of information technology is having an impact on all aspects of our daily life, many managers (and their departments) have a limited knowledge of information management and computers. To a great extent this is the legacy of the ways in which organisations once perceived their information needs – information storage was stressed rather than information for decision-making.

We have seen that information management should not be considered as something that is concerned solely with computers. Much of the work of frontline staff and managers means information is communicated verbally and through paper-based systems which are appropriate for the objectives at that level of the organisation. Nevertheless it is becoming increasingly important that managers and staff develop their skills in the use of computers which play an increasing role in information management.

Accessing information on services

One of the areas of rapid development that has been facilitated by information technology is the growth of websites that provide information to the public about their services. In some areas these are well developed; in others they are limited and difficult to use. If the NHS experience is a representative example (my NHS students tell me patients often have more information than clinicians from accessing websites), it is clear that users of services and carers will increasingly use computers to seek information. This will change the relationship between services and their users, as the power rooted in information is no longer held solely by professionals.

Internet

The internet is a huge network of computers that spans the globe and is a system that allows the exchange of information between computers. Because of the range of services available it is increasingly valuable as an information resource and communications superhighway. For example, it enables you to access thousands of databases at universities and research centres throughout the world, read electronic journals and exchange information, and send virtually instantaneous electronic mail (email) to any organisation or person connected to the internet.

The internet offers the frontline manager the potential to considerably expand their knowledge and understanding through access to websites which are designed specifically for social work and social care professionals, and of course the associated sites, such as those providing information on the NHS.

Access to, and the use of research is crucial to the development of services if action is to be based on hard information rather than hunches. Traditionally social care practitioners have been reluctant to engage with research, but with the advent of the internet it is possible to access current research through research centres' websites and to exchange information and views through newsgroups on a worldwide basis.

An enormous range of information is currently available, with the main access points for social care practitioners and managers through gateways at university and research centre websites (see **Appendix 1** for information on useful websites).

'Since I developed my skills in using the internet I've started accessing the Department of Health website and have been better informed about Government policy changes and also have also been able to keep staff informed. I'm no longer dependent on the department feeding information to me. I've often got the information before my manager!'

Residential services manager

Electronic mail (email)

Alongside the worldwide web, email is one of the main attractions of the internet. It allows for information exchange in the form of messages and (where necessary) attached correspondence, files, reports and graphics to be sent worldwide in seconds. It is a fast and effective way of communicating, within the service and externally. Its greatest value is its ability to send information and reports accurately and quickly, with replies often received within minutes.

Intranets

Many organisations are developing 'intranets' which are similar to the internet but are usually private and are restricted to staff from within a particular organisation which owns the intranet or other approved organisations. These systems are developing rapidly in the health service, where hospitals and community services staff can communicate rapidly on a range of information to speed up admission and discharge arrangements as well as diagnostic results. This type of information exchange using intranets will increasingly feature in all public services.

Developing your skills in information technology

You also need to develop your skills in computing as this is a skill that will become increasingly important for accessing knowledge which can help you make better quality decisions and enable you to transmit and receive information much more quickly than paper-based systems.
A further important skill is the use of the internet. This will enable you to access information that can help you in your decision-making.

Therefore, in terms of current operational requirements and in terms of longer term career development, it is in your interest that you become confident in the use of computers and that you see them as another tool that can assist you in effective management.

Much of what you can achieve in this area will be dependent on the information strategy developed by your organisation and on how far the department has progressed in training and supporting managers and other staff to develop competencies in the use of information technology.

Irrespective of the rate of progress in your service (and many managers told me of their frustration with the slow adoption of information technology to enable them to perform more effectively), there is much to be gained by taking the initiative and developing your skills in this area. This will enable you to comment critically on information management strategies from an informed perspective and to support new initiatives to enhance information systems.

KEY POINTS

○ An important skill is understanding what information you need to enable you to make decisions at the front line of the service.

○ Supporting staff who collect data from the front line play a crucial role in informing the service about current and emerging patterns of need. Supporting them to carry out that role is one of your main information management responsibilities.

○ In information terms you are the bridge between practice and management, which means you are located at the nexus of one of the most important communication points in the service.

○ All public services are adopting information management systems based on computers and you need to develop your skills in this area to make best use of this powerful information resource.

Managing work-based learning

Introduction

It is increasingly recognised that there needs to be much greater integration between the strategic objectives of social services departments and the development of staff to meet these objectives. With the advent of the Government's modernisation agenda, much greater emphasis is being placed on defining the competencies staff need to develop to improve the quality and responsiveness of services.

Establishing work-based learning: the frontline manager's role

Although many staff in social care agencies will have undertaken formal educational and training programmes to achieve professional qualifications, it is in the support of work-based learning that you have a critical influence. Michael Eraut(1998), discussing the findings of the Learning Society programme, states that of all the mechanisms used in organisations to promote learning, the most important is the appointment and development of managers and their influence on the service and approaches to learning.

Eraut's research also suggests that formal education and training provide only a small part of what is learned at work. Most learning was described by interviewees as informal, neither clearly specified nor planned, and arising naturally out of the demands and challenges of the work (eg solving problems, improving quality or productivity or coping with change) and out of social interactions with colleagues or clients. This work-based learning could nevertheless be enhanced when it was supported by a climate, created by the manager, to support and facilitate this informal learning.

Clearly, frontline managers are influential in a number of ways. Gerry Smale (1998) sees them as crucial opinion leaders who play a key role in any changes in practice or policy initiated by senior managers or by frontline staff in partnership with service users. Similarly, their professional behaviour affects staff, whose practice will be influenced by the standards you set for yourself and expect of others.

eg

Research by the National Institute for Social Work (2000) found that the main methods through which staff in social services departments acquired skills were from doing the job and working with more experienced people.

Assumptions in work-based learning

How you see your role in the management and facilitation of work-based learning will depend to a great extent on your management style and how much you value this aspect of your role.

Giles Darvill (1997) has identified some of the assumptions which underpin work-based learning, including:

- the quality and performance of staff can be raised by helping them to acquire an understanding and a sense of value and meaning of what they are doing

- the management of continuous learning is a major contribution to improving standards of practice

- learning what improves practice should incorporate a willingness to question habits, to experiment, to use time to reflect and to develop new ways of seeing

- managers need to make informed choices from the range of potential learning resources and learning processes. This means an awareness of the opportunities and resources available to help them with managing their own and others' continuous learning

- frontline managers have a number of key roles in relation to the continuous learning of staff, including managing the overall staff development processes for their team, contributing directly as a facilitator or coach and, importantly, setting examples as learners themselves.

Leadership in learning

Darvill sees you as possessing the most influence in promoting the vision of your team as a learning culture. You also have influence in adopting a strategic approach to the development of your team, establishing a clearer understanding of what the team is doing and how it could be improved for the benefit of service users. You also have an important role in setting an example as a learner. You can demonstrate this by:

- declaring the importance you place on your own learning
- identifying, with help where needed, your own learning needs
- asking difficult questions in supervision, team meetings, etc that question both your effectiveness and the effectiveness of other people and demonstrate a receptiveness to new ideas
- using formal and informal learning activities yourself.

Setting an example

In helping to create a learning climate in your organisation, model leadership in learning by:

- doing it yourself – always engage in learning something
- sharing and demonstrating your new learning – communicate with colleagues that you have learned something new
- making learning normal. Legitimate it and encourage others to do it – are colleagues around you learning from what they are doing?

But remember:

- don't feel under pressure to be competent all the time

- don't get into the position of never admitting to learning or needing to learn so that no one around you is willing to offer help.

Possible approaches in work-based learning

In order to support work-based learning it is important to understand that there is a range of possibilities available to staff. Again I have relied on Giles Darvill's helpful review of learning methods, some of which will be familiar to you, and others which are more specialised and require additional support and expertise.

- **Induction** – training provided for new staff or staff transferring to new roles.

- **Supervision** – seen as important in terms of supporting the learning needs of staff, and can incorporate training techniques as part of the supervision process. Darvill sees the training focus of supervision as useful in helping staff understand practice issues and in improving their skills.

- **Coaching** – showing staff directly how to carry out tasks, and providing close, reflective feedback on staff's work.

- **Mentoring** – mentoring has some overlap with supervision and coaching but is less role or task-specific. It is essentially about providing support (particularly from someone who is experienced) and can provide a wider perspective – the 'wise elder'. It has been developed in many organisations in relation to the development of managers, although frontline managers may increasingly be involved in mentoring staff who are using open learning materials or completing post-qualifying awards which are based on practice evidence from the workplace.

- **Assessor roles** – these are well developed in social work, with practice teaching as part of Diploma in Social Work courses and the assessment of National Vocational Qualifications in the workplace.

- **Team meetings** – these have the potential to be used as the basis for learning, particularly if they are facilitated by someone who does not have managerial authority for the team.

- **Inter-agency meetings** – the growing importance of partnership working opportunities to bring together staff from different agencies (sometimes using open learning materials) has a history going back to the community care implementation of the mid-1990s. Darvill sees the mixing of the groups as the most valued aspect of this manner of working.

- **Learning sets** – can be based on staff from one agency or from a number of agencies that meet to explore current problems and produce results based on analysis of the problem and problem-solving ideas. They require close attention to the contract between the members and to ground rules, issues of time and the commitment of members. Skilled facilitation can also enable the set to achieve its aims more effectively.

- **Consultancy** – usually refers to an external consultant who works alongside managers and staff to support the introduction of new policies or other initiatives. The objectivity and breadth of experience that the consultant offers is an important factor in the decision to engage someone from outside the organisation. Frontline managers often act in a consultancy role in their own teams, although it is helpful in some situations if the consultant does not have line management responsibility.

External resources

National Vocational Qualifications play an increasingly important role in social care agencies with the development of National Occupational Standards and the strategic development of the social care workforce. For staff in residential and day services NVQ care awards are now a well established part of the training available to staff and have also provided supervisory and frontline managers with the opportunity to train as assessors and to develop the relationship between occupational standards and the performance of staff. The role of NVQs in management has been more limited, although the increasing regulation of the social care workforce will soon see new requirements implemented – particularly for managers of residential and day services. As a frontline manager you have an important role as assessor as well as mentoring staff completing NVQs and day services leading to the 'Registered Managers' award.

Giles Darvill has also suggested that a further valuable aspect of NVQs is the use of elements and performance indicators as learning materials in their own right. The fact that portfolios are used to develop ideas for future planning and improvement of services (rather than purely to demonstrate current staff performance) is also regarded as valuable.

Open and distance learning materials

These materials have a range of applications including training in-service and in educational courses. They also provide opportunities for staff to access study when they cannot attend traditional courses and can be used to support group activities such as learning sets. The MESOL texts are good examples of the new range of high quality, open learning materials which can be used in a range of ways by social services departments and other social care agencies.

Qualifying and post-qualifying awards

The Diploma in Social Work in its employment-based, part-time mode offers opportunities for staff to undertake training and development while remaining in employment, and is important in meeting the needs of staff who are unable to undertake full-time courses. Similarly, qualified staff have access to an increasing range of post-qualifying training tailored to the needs of social services departments, with opportunities on some courses to achieve both academic and CCETSW post-qualifying and advanced award credits through local CCETSW credit rating arrangements. CCETSW awards can also be achieved entirely within the workplace through portfolio-based routes.

National developments in staff training

The major development that you need to be aware of is the work of the National Training Organisation for the Personal Social Services (TOPSS) which is engaged in developing the first national training strategy for the social care workforce.

TOPSS is establishing a national qualifications framework based on competencies and underpinned by a map of National Occupation Standards. The National Occupational Standards in Care are being developed as a central part of this work, with the intention of providing a training and workforce strategy which will identify the workforce requirements in terms of numbers of staff, the skill mix for particular tasks and a framework of qualifications based on National Occupational Standards. It is intended that National Occupational Standards will eventually cover all jobs within social care services.

These standards will provide the practice benchmarks for services and will be used for job definitions, skills assessment and audit, and the development of training activities and performance appraisal. They will also provide support for the frontline manager in identifying the core competencies staff should be able to demonstrate in relation to practice tasks, and in supporting the developmental focus of staff supervision.

Increasingly, training will be linked to the National Qualifications Framework based on occupational standards. These standards will be used as the basis for vocational qualifications, and as a frontline manager you will be expected to develop assessment skills in order to support staff who are using relevant standards as the basis for achieving vocational qualifications.

The TOPSS publication *Modernising the Social Care Workforce – the first national training strategy for England* (1999) is important reading for frontline managers whose training and developments role is central to supporting the development of a more skilled and competent workforce.

KEY POINTS

○ You are in a position as frontline manager to play a crucial role in promoting and supporting work-based learning opportunities.

○ Your own approach to learning can be influential in creating a wider commitment to learning.

○ There is a wide range of work-based learning methods that you can use to develop individuals and teams.

○ National Occupational Standards and the role of competencies are growing in importance in services.

Managing your own development

Introduction

The concern to improve the quality of management in social care agencies is evident from statements, for example from the Chief Inspector of Social Services (1999) and the Audit Commission (1998), about the importance of the role of frontline managers and the need for a much more structured approach to the training and development needs of managers.

Management as a unique activity

John Burgoyne (1999) has described management as an activity that is concerned primarily with uncertainty in organisations. This has important implications for what managers need to learn. He describes managing as dealing with the messy problems that are left when those tasks that can be dealt with by routine, specialist, technical and professional work are removed.

It is this messiness which makes management different from the point of view of learning. The learning and development needed to prepare managers for unprogrammed work is different from the learning applied to routine problems. The management role calls for a range of human abilities, including creativity, judgement, intelligence and insight. These abilities are the generally less specific, and are 'developed' rather than acquired through training.

What is management development?

Burgoyne's view of management means that approaches to development need to encompass a wide range of opportunities. These should include formal activities such as training programmes and courses but also mentoring and coaching, and access to programmed learning resources and open learning materials. At its heart, management development should be an integral part of management and concerned with how you can improve your effectiveness and the performance of the organisation using learning processes applied to all aspects of your work.

Organisational commitment to management development

How your organisation responds to your learning and development needs will depend to a great extent on its strategy for developing its staff and the integration of staff development with its corporate goals.

According to John Burgoyne, the greater the degree of integration between the development of strategy and corporate management development, the more likely it is that managers will be able to meet the challenge of implementing the organisation's strategy. The reverse of this is for the organisation to develop strategies that managers (and others) do not have the competence to implement. (Many managers have described the implementation of strategies as the Achilles heel of their organisation.) Burgoyne sees the two-way process between management development policy and corporate strategy creating the link between individual and organisational learning.

Role of training and development in organisations

Kevin Barham and colleagues (1988) developed what has become known as the Ashridge model which is helpful in identifying the role of training and development in organisations. Ideally, organisations should be moving towards what they describe as a focused approach, with training and development supporting the strategic development of the organisation.

The focused approach

- Training and development, and continuous development, are seen as necessary for organisations' survival in a rapidly changing environment.
- Learning is linked to organisational strategy and to individual goals.
- Emphasis is on role development so that learning is a continuous activity.
- New forms of training are used – open and distance learning, self-development packages etc.
- The effectiveness of training and development is measured.
- The main responsibility for training rests with line management.
- Managers are trained to adopt a wider consultancy and adviser role.

ACTIVITY

1. How far has your organisation embraced a focused approach to training and development?

   ....

   ....

   ....

2. Are the sort of activities described by Barham and colleagues present in your organisation?

   ....

   ....

   ....

3. If not, what do you need to do to ensure that your learning and development needs are met?

   ....

   ....

   ....

Self-assessment of your management skills

A useful starting point for thinking about your training and development needs is to identify your performance across a range of typical management activities in order to identify specific areas where you need to develop your skills. This can then be used in discussions with your line manager and with training and development advisers. Although the checklist is based on self-appraisal, it is helpful to widen your assessment to include your line manager and peers.

Including your line manager in self-assessment

As we have seen in the chapter on work-based learning (**Chapter 13**), managers have a significant influence on the development of their staff's learning. It is therefore important to engage with your line manager in discussing your learning needs.

Photocopy the checklist (see over) for your line manager and ask for feedback about your skills, which you can then use to complement your own self-assessment.

Including your peers and colleagues in self-assessment

It can also be useful to extend the assessment of your skills to include peers and colleagues if you feel they will be helpful and truthful in their scoring. You need first to discuss the reasons why you are using the checklist and why their assessment of your management skills would be helpful. Again, photocopy the checklist for your colleagues to complete.

Remember that the checklist shows just a selection of potential questions and that you will need to take account of your particular role and work setting. Ignore those that are not relevant to your role and add to the list in the spaces provided other items that you feel are important. Once you have completed the checklist your scores will give you pointers to your training and development needs and suggest skills you may need to develop. If you have asked other people to complete the checklist, what do their assessments of your management skills suggest?

ACTIVITY

Self-assessment checklist

This activity is concerned with assessing your current level of competence and does not attempt to be all-embracing. Rate yourself against each item using the scale below:

1. Lacking competence in this area (know little about this area or experience extreme difficulty).

2. Do not feel competent in this area (experience difficulty, although not without some knowledge and/or skill).

3. Competent in this area (feel competent in this area, but occasionally experience some difficulty).

4. Very competent in this area (maintain a consistently high level of performance).

Circle the appropriate number

Managing yourself

1.	Set personal work objectives	I	2	3	4
2.	Review and monitor objectives	I	2	3	4
3.	Communicate your values	I	2	3	4
4.	Respond assertively	I	2	3	4
5.	Handle criticism	I	2	3	4
6.	Effectively manage your time	I	2	3	4
7.	Express your feelings	I	2	3	4
8.	Adapt your management style to suit the situation	I	2	3	4
9.	Manage pressure	I	2	3	4
10.	Manage your own stress	I	2	3	4
11.	Take a 'helicopter' objective view	I	2	3	4
12.	Create and use learning opportunities	I	2	3	4
13.	Process data and information quickly	I	2	3	4
14.	Evaluate and change your own performance	I	2	3	4
15.		I	2	3	4
16.		I	2	3	4
17.		I	2	3	4

Managing others

1.	Relate well to staff at all levels	I	2	3	4
2.	Sensitive to others' values	I	2	3	4

Continued…

		1	2	3	4
3.	Recognise the feelings of others	1	2	3	4
4.	Give clear instructions	1	2	3	4
5.	Assess the performance of staff	1	2	3	4
6.	Counsel and coach staff	1	2	3	4
7.	Use confrontation constructively	1	2	3	4
8.	Use appropriate listening skills	1	2	3	4
9.	Persuade and influence people	1	2	3	4
10.	Demand high standards of yourself and others	1	2	3	4
11.	Gain group support	1	2	3	4
12.	Negotiate constructively between competing views	1	2	3	4
13.	Keep group discussion 'on task'	1	2	3	4
14.	Close a group effectively	1	2	3	4
15.	Give feedback constructively	1	2	3	4
16.	Build on the contribution of others	1	2	3	4
17.	Encourage appropriate participation	1	2	3	4
18.	Delegate clearly	1	2	3	4
19.	Manage meetings	1	2	3	4
20.	Communicate information effectively – verbal and written	1	2	3	4
21.	Gather information	1	2	3	4
22.	Present information	1	2	3	4

Managing the service

		1	2	3	4
1.	Set objectives and identify priorities	1	2	3	4
2.	Review performance	1	2	3	4
3.	Design and implement procedures	1	2	3	4
4.	Use communication and information systems	1	2	3	4
5.	Manage your budget	1	2	3	4
6.	Identify quality standards	1	2	3	4
7.	Measure the quality of services provided	1	2	3	4
8.	Work with other agencies	1	2	3	4
9.	Manage organisational change	1	2	3	4
10.	Promote your service	1	2	3	4
11.		1	2	3	4
12.		1	2	3	4
13.		1	2	3	4

(Adapted from: Broome, 1990; Barlow, 1990)

ACTIVITY

Self-assessment – setting priorities

My training and development priorities for the next 6 months are:

....

....

....

....

My training and development priorities for the next 6–12 months are:

....

....

....

....

The future of social care: implications for frontline managers' self-development

An important part of managing your own development is to understand how the future will be different from the past. Organisational life is changing rapidly, in terms both of structures and processes. A recent report from a group of training managers (MESOL, 2000) and thinking from the SSI Leadership Development Event suggests what the social care world will look like in the future. It identifies some of drivers for change, including:

- Best Value
- performance assessment
- outcome orientation
- service user focus
- enhanced arrangements for partnership
- a focus on the health of communities.

It suggests that these changes will be achieved through:

- much greater integration of services across local authority departments
- stronger partnerships, leading to greater integration with health services
- continuing reduction in direct service provision by local authorities and strengthening of the commissioning role
- increased provision by private and voluntary sectors.

To achieve these changes the group identifies some requirements:

- training will need to embrace a more strategic approach to learning and development
- occupational standards should play an important part with the specification of core competencies for managers at different levels
- skills of reflection should be developed (which are important for managers in some organisations who can get into the habit of frantic action)
- cross-boundary developments between organisations should be encouraged, with the new emphasis on partnership-working providing new opportunities
- the accumulated competence and experience of managers should be accredited, which will require more sophisticated accreditation processes.

These changes will have considerable consequences for you in your frontline role and you need to think increasingly carefully about your career development, where some of the traditional assumptions about career advancement are likely to be questioned. You will need to be better informed about developmental opportunities and keep a strong focus on your own development needs. To help you focus on these needs, ask yourself the following questions:

- what are the implications of these projected changes for your development?
- what do you need to think about in terms of your own career development?
- what areas of development do you need to emphasise?
- where will you be able to get the help you need?

Getting support for your development in the face of change

Make a list of stakeholders who can support you in your career and personal development, for example:

- your line manager
- your colleagues who are in management or management development roles
- human resource specialists.

Talk to them about what you want, and what you should be learning so that you are able to identify:

- what opportunities are available and likely to become available in the future
- what services they offer
- what use you can make of them

...and remember to behave assertively about your development. Specialists will welcome this and encourage you as this will help them match the needs of managers to the organisation's needs.

ACTIVITY

Below are listed some helpful questions that managers can use when planning for their development (Cunningham, 1994). Try answering the following, writing down your thoughts on a sheet of paper.

1. Where have I been? (What is my background, previous experience?)
2. Where am I now? (What knowledge and skills do I possess?)
3. Where do I want to get to? (What kind of skills do I want to develop?)
4. How do I get there?
5. What learning processes or programmes do I need? (What processes can I go through in order to learn?)
6. How will I know when I have arrived? (How will I evaluate my learning?)

Ian Cunningham suggests that this exercise is ideally carried out with others, particularly those who are engaged in similar planning processes, as the collaboration can help you improve your own processes.

Identifying learning opportunities

Chapter 13 on work-based learning lists a wide range of approaches that can be used when responding to staff's needs. These same approaches are equally relevant to managers. In fact some of them, such as mentoring and action learning, have a long history in management development.

You should explore the different approaches potentially available to you, ideally with an experienced management development adviser. This will allow you to identify those learning opportunities which best fit your own preferred ways of working and personal circumstances. It will also help you establish what is practical in terms of access and participation in development activities both within the work setting and through external educational and training programmes. Managers interviewed for this handbook suggested that the ideal activity combined both vocational and academic elements, providing space to reflect on the complexity of management in a social care setting and also offering practical ideas that can be tested out in the workplace.

KEY POINTS

○ Organisations need to integrate the development of managers with their wider strategic development so that implementation can be successful.

○ It can be helpful to carry out a self-assessment of your current skills and ask others to rate your skills in order to provide a baseline for discussing your training and development needs.

○ Contact management development advisers or training staff with an interest in this field and discuss how they can support you in meeting your development needs.

○ Learn about the range of learning opportunities available to managers and choose those that suit your personal approach to learning and will prepare you for the future.

○ The social care sector is changing rapidly and you need to reflect on the changes and the implications on your career.

Adair, J. (1988) *Effective Leadership*. London: Pan Books.

Adair, J. (1987) *Effective Teambuilding*. London: Pan Books.

Audit Commission 1998, *Better by Far: Preparing for Best Value.* Abingdon: Audit Commission.

Babbington-Smith, B. & Farrell, B. A. (1979) *Training in Small Groups.* Oxford: Pergamon.

Balloch, S., Andrew, T., Ginn, J., McLean, J., Pahl, J. & Williams, J. (1995) *Working in Social Services.* London: National Institute for Social Work.

Bamford, T. (1982) *Managing Social Work*. London: Tavistock Publications.

Barham, K., Fraser, J. & Heath, L. (1988) *Management for the Future.* Berkhamstead: Foundation for Management Research and Ashridge Management College.

Barlow, A. (Ed) (1990) *Transitions: A self assessment and development package for managers in social services*. Luton: Local Government Management Board.

Barrett, P. (1987) Teambuilding. In: D. M. Stewart (Ed) *Handbook of Management Skills*. Aldershot: Golder.

Broome, A. (1990) *Managing Change*. Basingstoke: Macmillan.

Browning, D. (2000) *The Way to Go Home: Rehabilitation and remedial services for older people.* Abingdon: Audit Commission.

Burgoyne, J. (1999) *Developing Yourself, Your Career and Your Organization.* London: Lemos and Crane.

Burns, J. M. (1978) *Leadership*. London: Harper and Row.

Caple, T. (1990) *Preparing People for Change: A handbook for trainers and managers*. Bristol: National Health Service Training Authority.

Clode, D., Ethrington, S., Munchou, J. & Peck, E. (1993) *The Essential Manager in Health and Social Care: Improving management skills in health and social care.* Brighton: Pavilion.

Coulshed, V. (1990) *Management in Social Work.* Basingstoke: Macmillan.

Cunningham, I. (1994) *The Wisdom of Strategic Learning: The self managed solution.* London: McGraw-Hill.

Darvill, G. (Ed.) (1995) *The Changing Needs of First-Line Managers and Middle Managers in the Personal Social Services: Report of a Seminar, 6th July 1995.* London: National Institute for Social Work and the Association of Directors of Social Services.

Darvill, G. (1997) *The Management of Work-Based Learning: A guide for managers of social care and social work on raising standards of practice.* London: The Stationery Office.

Darvill, G. (1997) *Directory of Materials on Management Development.* London: National Institute for Social Work.

Darvill, G. (1998) *Organisation, People and Standards: Use of formal standards in social services, report of a survey.* London: National Institute for Social Work.

Drucker, P. (1974) *Management: Tasks, responsibilities, practice.* London: Heinemann.

Eraut, M. (1998) Managers hold the key to developing knowledge and skills. *Professional Manager* 7 (2) 41.

Farrell, C., Robinson, J. & Fletcher, P. (1999) *A New Era for Community Care? What people want from health, housing and social care services.* London: King's Fund.

Field, R (1999) Budgeting is simple: It's management that is difficult! *Management Issues in Social Care* 6 (1) 1–6.

Ford, K. & Hargreaves, S. (1991) *First Line Management: Staff.* Brighton: Pavilion.

Hackman, J. R. & Oldham, G. (1980) *Work Redesign.* Massachusetts: Addison-Wesley.

Hales, C. (1993) *Managing through Organisation.* London: Routledge.

Handy, C. (1999) *Understanding Organisations* (4th edition). Harmondsworth: Penguin.

Harris, J. & Kelly, D. (1992) *Management Skills in Social Care: A Handbook for Social Care Managers.* Aldershot: Ashgate.

Hawkins, P. & Shohet, R. (1990) *Supervision in the Helping Professions.* Milton Keynes: Open University Press.

Hearn, B., Darvill, G. & Morris, B.(Eds)(1992) *On Becoming a Manager in Social Work.* Harlow: Longman.

Harvard Business Review (January –February) 53–62

Herzberg, F. (1974) *Work and the Nature of Man?* London: Granada Publishing.

Hudson, M. (1995) *Managing Without Profit: The art of managing third sector organizations.* London: Penguin.

Jeffrey, J. (1996) Information management and technology: Making sure you benefit from IT. In: A. Kerslake and N. Gould (Eds) *Information Management in Social Services.* Aldershot: Avebury.

Johnson, M., Gillan, L. & Patsior, D. (1999) *Managers in Long-Term Care: their quality and qualities.* Bristol: Policy Press in association with The Joseph Rowntree Foundation.

Jones, B. (1996) *Financial Management in the Public Sector.* London: McGraw-Hill.

Kakabadse, A., Ludlow, R. & Vinnicombe, S. (1988) *Working in Organisations.* London: Penguin.

Kearney, P. (Ed) (1999) *Managing Practice: Project report.* London: National Institute for Social Work.

King's Fund (1999) *A New Era for Community Care? What people want from health, housing and social care services.* London: King's Fund.

Knapman, J. & Morrison, T. (1998) *Making the Most of Supervision in Health and Social Care: A self-development manual for supervisees*. Brighton: Pavilion.

Lawler, J. & Hearn, J. (1997) The managers of social work: the experiences and identification of third tier social services managers and the implications for future practice. *British Journal of Social Work* **27 (2)** 191–218.

Martin, V. (2000) *Managing in Health and Social Care*. Milton Keynes: The Open University.

Maslow, A. (1987) *Motivation and Personality* (3rd edition). New York: Harper and Row.

MESOL (2000) *Managing in Health and Social Care*. Milton Keynes: The Open University.

MESOL (2000) The SSI Leadership Development Initiative: Preparing for the world of 2005. *MESOL Update* **21**(3) 3.

Mintzberg, H. (1990) The Manager's Job: Folklore and fact. *Harvard Business Review* (March–April) 163–176.

Morrison, T. (1996) *Staff Supervision in Social Care*. Brighton: Pavilion.

Morrison, T., Waters, J., Roberts, W., Craig, E. & Shearer, E. (1987) *Surviving in Teams*. Rochdale: Rochdale NSPCC Child Protection Team.

Mullins, L. (1996) *Management and Organisational Behaviour* (4th edition). London: Pitman Publishing.

National Health Service Training Directorate (1993) *Managing Service Partnerships*. Bristol: NHSTD.

National Institute for Social Work (2000) The social services workforce in transition. (Research Summary **13** pp1–8).

Open College (1992) *Public Sector Management*. Warrington: Open College.

Page, K. & Gilder, P. (2000) Developing financial management in a social work department. *Management Issues in Social Care* **7** (2) 23–25.

Palmer, P. & Papaiacovou, C. (1992) *Managing Budgets in Health and Social Care*. Brighton: Pavilion.

Richards, M. & Payne, C. (1990) *Staff Supervision in Child Protection Work*. London: National Institute for Social Work.

Rosen, G. (Ed) (1999) *Managing Team Development: A short guide for teams and team managers*. London: National Institute for Social Work.

Rosen, G. (Ed) (2000) *Integrity, the Organisation and the First-Line Manager: Discussion papers*. London: National Institute for Social Work.

Scragg, T. (1995) *Providing for Care: A manual for managers of social care services*. Brighton: Pavilion.

Shanahan, P. (1999) *Managing Information: Health and social services management*. Milton Keynes: The Open University.

Shanahan, P. (1999) *Managing Information: Book 1: Information in the support of care*. MESOL Health and Social Services Management. Milton Keynes: Open University.

Smale, G. (1998) *Managing Change through Innovation*. London: The Stationery Office.

Social Services Inspectorate (1997) *Informing Care: Inspection of social service department information strategies and systems*. London: Social Services Inspectorate.

Social Services Inspectorate (1999) *Modern Social Service: A commitment to improve, 8th report of the Chief Inspector of Social Services, 1998/1999*. London: Department of Health.

Stevenson, O. & Parsloe, P. (1978) *Social Services Teams: The practitioner's view*. London: HSMO.

Stewart, R. (1997) *The Reality of Management* (3rd edition). Oxford: Butterworth-Heinemann.

Tannerbaum, R. & Schmidt, W. H. (1973) How to choose a leadership pattern. *Harvard Business Review* (May–June) 162–175.

TOPSS (1999) *Modernising the Social Care Workforce: The first national training strategy for England*. Leeds: TOPSS England.

Wheatley, R. & Smith, C. (1995) *Leadership*. Corby: Institute of Management.

Useful books, materials, journals and websites

Government policy documents

Modern Social Services: A commitment to improve, The 8th report of the Chief Inspector of Social Services (1998/1999). London: Department of Health.

Modernising Social Services (1998). London: The Stationery Office.

Books on management in social work and social care

Bamford, T. (1982) *Managing Social Work.* London: Tavistock Publications.

Cockburn, J. (1990) *Team Leaders and Team Managers in Social Services.* Norwich: University of East Anglia.

Coulshed, V. & Mullender A.(2000) *Management in Social Work* (2nd edition). Basingstoke: Palgrave.

Cypher, J. (Ed) (1982) *Team Leadership in the Social Services.* Birmingham: BASW.

Department of Health (1998) *National Service Frameworks.* London: Department of Health.

Harris, J. & Kelly, D. (1992) *Management Skills in Social Care.* Aldershot: Ashgate.

Hearn, B., Darvill, G. & Morris, B. (1992) *On Becoming a Manager in Social Work.* Harlow: Longman.

Note: Some of these books are now out of print, but are still useful reading for frontline (and other) managers. Try to obtain out of print books through your local library, or order through the British Library Inter-Library Loans Scheme.

Managing not-for-profit organisations

Hudson, M. (1995) *Managing Without Profit: The art of managing third-sector organizations.* London: Penguin.

Books on general management

Handy, C. (1999) *Understanding Organisations* (4th edition). London: Penguin.

Kakabadse, A., Ludlow, R. & Vinnicombe, S. (1988) *Working in Organisations.* London: Penguin.

Mullins, L. (1996) *Management and Organisational Behaviour* (4th edition). London: Pitman Publishing.

Management of Practice

The Management of Practice Expertise is three booklets based on the Management of Practice Expertise project conducted by the National Institute for Social Work.

Managing Team Development: A short guide for teams and team managers.

Managing Practice: Report on the management of practice expertise project.

Integrity, the Organisation and the First Line Manager.

All available from NISW.

Staff supervision

Knapman, J. & Morrison, T. (2001) *Making the Most of Supervision in Health and Social Care: A self-development manual for supervisees* (2nd edition). Brighton: Pavilion.

Morrison, T. (1999) *Staff Supervision in Social Care.* Brighton: Pavilion.

Work-based learning

Darvil, G. (1997)*The Management of Work-Based Learning: A guide for managers of social care and social work on raising standards of practice.* London: HMSO.

Training and development

Modernising the Social Care Workforce: First national training strategy for England, consultation document. (1999) London: TOPSS.

Management Development, consultation document. (1999) London: TOPSS.

Open Learning materials

The Management Education Scheme by Open Learning produces materials for managers containing workbooks that can be studied independently or in association with MESOL centres in universities and some health and social services departments.

MESOL (2000) *The Health and Social Services Manager.* Milton Keynes: OU.

MESOL (1999) *Managing in Health and Social Care.* Milton Keynes: OU.

Contact: MESOL National Office
NHS Leadership Centre
2nd Floor
Room 212 Gateway House
Piccadilly South
Manchester M60 7LP
Telephone: 0161 237 2992/2332
Fax: 0161 237 2398
email: admin@mesol.org.uk

National Institute for Social Work

Services include:
- Individual Membership Scheme
- NISW Caredata Abstracts (including online version)
- Policy briefings
- Research Summaries
- Noticeboard Publications

Contact: National Institute for Social Work
5 Tavistock Place
London WC1 9SN
Telephone: 020 7387 9681
Fax: 020 7387 7968
email: info@nisw.org.uk

Journals

British Journal of Social Work
Telephone: 01865 267907
Fax: 01865 267485
email: jnlorders@oup.co.uk
Website: www.bjsw.oupjournals.org

Community Care
Freepost RCC 2619
Haywards Heath   RH16 3BR
Telephone: 01444 445566
Fax: 01444 445599
Website: www.community-care.co.uk

Health Services Journal
Tower Publishing Services Ltd
Tower House
Sovereign Park
Market Harborough LE16 9EF
Telephone: 01858 438847
Website: www.hsj.co.uk

The Kent Journal of Practice Research, Canterbury
Kent Social Services Research Strategy Group
Department of Social Work
Canterbury Christ Church College
North Holmes Road
Canterbury CT1 1QU
Telephone: 01227 782410
Website: www.cant.ac.uk/depts/aced/social/kjpr/

Managing Community Care
Pavilion
The Ironworks
Cheapside
Brighton BN1 4GD
Telephone: 01273 623222
Fax: 01273 625526
email: info@pavpub.com
Website: www. pavpub.com

Management Issues in Social Care
OLM Consulting Ltd
Howard House Commercial Centre
Howard Streeet
North Shields   NE30 1AR
Telephone: 0191 296 5333

Community Care Research Matters
Freepost RCC 2619
Reed Business Information
Haywards Heath RH16 3BR
Telephone (subscriptions): 01444 445566
email: rbc.subscriptions@rbc.co.uk
Website www. reed business.com/subscribe/research_matters.asap

Websites

The **Audit Commission** website lists activities and publications, including joint reviews of social services departments.
www.audit-commission.gov.uk

The **Joseph Rowntree Foundation** website contains information on current research projects and abstracts from publications.
www. jrf.org.uk

Best practice: The Government's Quality Protects website is an example of a website devoted to providing managers and practitioners with information on best practice.
www.doh.gov.uk/quality.htm

The **British Association of Social Workers** site has information on the work of BASW and publications.
www. basw.co.uk

The **Care*and*health guide** is concerned with continuous professional development for all staff in the social work and social care professions. It includes brief information on current policy issues, guides to new legislation and current vacancies in social care. It is available both by email and as a paper copy. Order from the website.
www.careandhealth.com

The **Department of Health (Social Care Group)** has an extensive website containing a wide range of publications, including White Papers, policy statements, press releases etc.
www. doh.gov.uk/scg/socialc.htm

The **Centre for Evidence-Based Social Services**. The Exeter University website has information on the work of CEBSS and summaries of recent publications.
www. ex.ac.uk/cebss

Government web links. The Government public information site with direct web links to all central and many local government web links, including the Department of Health and the Audit Commission.
www.open.gov.uk

Improvement and development agency (IDeA). Publications on local government, including social services.
www.idea.gov.uk

Local Government Association (LGA). Publications on local government including social services.
www.lga.gov.uk

The Local Government site has summaries and full reports of policies for local government.
www. local.doe.gov.uk

Management Education Scheme by Open Learning (MESOL). Open learning materials for health and social services managers.
www.mesol.org.uk

National Institute for Social Work website listing publications, latest research findings and summaries of all publications.
www. nisw.org.uk

Online Netskills Interactive Course. A course of instruction for using the Internet.
www.netskills.ac.uk/TonicNG/cgi/sesame?tng

Pavilion produces training materials for social services managers, practitioners and training personnel, and journals of interest to social services managers. Abstracts are available on their website and sample copies of journals can be ordered from samplecopy@pavpub.com
Website: www.pavpub.com

Social Services Strategic Planning is the website of Keith Fletcher's consultancy company, with articles on Best Value and other topics of interest to social services managers.
www.ssp.demon.co.uk

The Southampton University Centre for Human Technology site, with its emphasis on information technology, has access to the Social Work Gateway with dozens of sites relevant to social work/social care.
www.soton.ac.uk/~chst/webconn.htm

Strathclyde University. The Wired Social Worker site and access to many other sites.
www.strath.ac.uk

The Training Organisation for the Personal Social Services site contains information on TOPSS, with reports on training strategies, including full reports.
www. topss.org.uk

Glossary of management and related terms

This glossary is intended as an aid to staff, particularly managers who are newly appointed to frontline posts who may be unfamiliar with some of the terminology used by colleagues in social services and other services. It offers definitions of basic terms and concepts used in relation to management of services.

Accreditation

a process by which an external body evaluates and recognises a service as meeting predetermined standards.

Action learning

a process where a group of staff from one or more organisations meet together with a facilitator to discuss and learn about work-based problems that they are charged with resolving.

Agency

any organisation – statutory, voluntary or private – which provides a social care service.

Arm's length

the idea of separating units which provide a service from the management of the department: for example, inspection units.

Assessment of performance

an analysis of performance against planned objectives taking account of all relevant factors.

Audit

the internal scrutiny of systems of control, and the external view of probity designed to ensure optimum use of resources.

Audit Commission

a body statutorily charged with the external audit of the public sector and in particular encouraged to search for value for money.

Auditors

those who audit compliance with quality standards, systems and procedures.

Base budget

the previous year's approved budget, adjusted for inflation, savings, commitments and known policy changes.

Benchmarking

assessing the competencies of a service against the 'best in class', wherever that is found.

Best value

the duty to deliver services to clear standards, covering both cost and quality, by the most economic, efficient and effective means available. (Audit Commission, 1998)

Billing authority

the council responsible for sending out council bills – in county areas this is the district or borough council.

Block contract

a contract negotiated with a provider for a large volume of a specified service.

BS5750 (ISO 9000)

an international standard which examines the quality of an organisation in terms of its fitness for purpose and safety in use. BS5750 was originally developed for use in the manufacturing sector and has been adapted for use in the service sector.

Budget

a plan prepared in advance for an operational period. It expresses the performance to be achieved during that period in financial or quantitative terms.

Budgetary control

a process of financial control. It uses the target of desired performance as its standard, then collates information relating to actual performance (usually on a monthly or four-week basis) and identifies variances between target and actual performance. The analysis of the variances enable action to be taken to correct or control significant variances.

Budget holder

an individual within an organisation who has authority to use a specific part of budget funds and the responsibility to account for the results.

Business plan

a general statement of objectives of the organisation and how available resources will be used to achieve those objectives.

Capital spending

spending on assets of long-term value such as buildings, and the structural maintenance of those assets.

Care management

the process of co-ordinating, managing and reviewing the care of an individual to ensure that it meets that individual's assessed needs.

Care package

the combination of services designed to meet a person's assessed needs.

Charters

statements of standards, committing an organisation to specific levels of quality. Developed in the public sector as in the Local Government and Patient's Charters.

Competence

the ability to perform work activities to expected standards. It is also used to describe where knowledge, skills and understanding come together in an individual's performance.

Commissioning

securing and monitoring services to meet individuals' needs. Commissioning is more commonly used to describe the strategic, long-term process by which this takes place as opposed to the short-term, operational, purchasing process.

Contingency provision

provision made for the anticipated pay and price inflation during the forth-coming financial year, which is allocated to service budgets as appropriate.

Control

the process of monitoring events, comparing them with the plan and taking appropriate action.

Contract

a legally binding agreement between a purchaser and provider through which a provider contacts to provide a service and the purchaser to pay for it.

Corporate management

a way of organising the management of an organisation which seeks to enhance the articulation and realisation of goals covering the whole organisation rather than its constituent parts.

Cost centre

a service, or part of a service, the cost of which can be separated, quantified, managed and related to the service provided. Also a convenient heading under which to gather costs, usually a department or part of a service.

Deficit

the equivalent of a loss: that is, excess of expenditure over income.

Delegation

giving someone else responsibility and authority to carry out a task.

Direct costs

items of expenditure which can easily be identified as belonging to a particular cost centre or activity.

Devolved responsibility

usually refers to a cost centre, with specified financial autonomy and responsibility.

Eligibility criteria

devices used to control and ration access to assessment and service provision where departments set out conditions which individuals have to meet before qualifying for services.

email

electronic mail, sent through a network from one computer screen to another computer screen. Almost instantaneous communication.

Enabling authority

a term used to describe a social services department which does not provide all services itself, but provides a framework of decision, regulation and payment which enables outside organisations to provide services.

Evaluation

the systematic process of determining the extent to which a programme or intervention achieves predetermined objectives.

Favourable variance

a difference between actual and budgeted spending or income which results in the organisation having more money than planned.

Fixed cost

the cost of a service which is independent of the level of service provided. Examples would be the rent of a building or equipment.

Gross spending

total level of spending before deducting income from fees, grants for specific purposes etc. (See also **Net expenditure.**)

Incremental budgeting

budget-making using the current budget as the starting point for determining the budget for the next time period.

Independent sector

privately owned and voluntary not-for-profit organisations.

Inflation

cost increases arising from pay settlements and price rises on other goods and services. Income is also subject to inflation.

Investors in People

a national standard which encourages an organisation to develop processes which train and develop all staff as a key resource to achieve its corporate goals.

IT or information technology

the term covering all the hardware (computers and printers) and software (computer programmes such as word processing, spreadsheets and databases) used in storing, processing and communicating information.

Joint commissioning

part of the purchasing function where an overall strategy, by all those organisations involved, is developed and agreed regarding the needs to meet within a population and the processes and resources for meeting those needs.

Joint reviews

independent reviews of the performance of social services departments by the Audit Commission and the Social Services Inspectorate. Intended to give a view of how a department is responding to individuals who need help, how it plans for its population and how it uses its resources.

Learning organisation

'an organisation that facilitates the learning of all its members and consciously transforms itself and its context' (Burgoyne, 1999).

Managing the market

using contracting and other processes to influence the supply of services to achieve commissioning strategy objectives.

Mapping the market

the process of identifying and analysing the factors influencing the existing and likely future demand for, and the supply of, care services to inform commissioning plans.

Management information system

a system using a network of computers linked to a central large computer and database, used for accessing, storing, processing and communicating management information within a service.

MESOL

Management Education Scheme by Open Learning. Open/distance learning materials designed to be used by managers in health and social care services as part of in-house, university or individual study means (see **Appendix 1**, page 173).

Mission statement

a generalised statement of the over-riding purpose of the organisation/a statement that defines why a service exists, its purpose and what it will attempt to achieve.

Mixed economy of care

the use of independent sector providers alongside public services to increase the range of available service options.

Monitoring

scrutinising activities and the results and expenditure and comparing information provided by others with planned objectives.

National Service Standards

any nationally required standards governing service provision.

National Vocational Qualifications

qualifications relevant to employment which recognise the achievement of performance as defined in statements of competence.

Net expenditure

the level of spending after deducting income from fees, grants for specific purposes etc. (See also **Gross expenditure.**)

Occupational standards

describe what has been agreed by representatives of employers to be the benchmark for the assessment of competent performance in the workplace.

On cost

an element, often expressed as a percentage, added to the cost of a service to cover indirect costs or overheads.

Open learning

a general term to describe a programme of study that is accessible to people who cannot follow traditional educational courses requiring attendance at colleges or where courses are not available. It is also provides flexibility for the learner to control the pace of progress through a course of training, including attendance, reading and tutor contact. Open learning is usually based on distance learning materials (see **MESOL**).

Out-turn

the final figures for income and/or expenditure at the end of an accounting period, normally the financial year.

Overheads

costs relating to the whole organisation which cannot easily be traced to any particular activity within it: for example, general administration.

Paradigm

a set of assumptions held generally and taken for granted in an organisation.

Performance assessment framework (PAF)

indicators covering all aspects of performance in social service departments. Used to monitor how performance is being maintained and improved, and to assist in the analysis of how Government policy is being implemented.

Performance indicator

a figure which is used internally or externally as a comparative measure of success. Some indicators relate to the costs of a service, others to the volume supplied and others to measures of quality and user satisfaction (see PAF).

Performance management

a process whereby individual or team performance is assessed so that judgements can be made about whether the work of staff is contributing to the effectiveness and efficiency of the service in relation to its stated aims.

Performance measures

criteria such as standards, specifications and benchmarks, by which to judge an organisation's performance.

Primary care trusts

new organisations consisting of general practitioners, community nurses and other health and social care professionals, who will commission, purchase and provide services in the community. The intention is that these services will bring together primary and community health services and social services to develop joint commissioning and greater integration of service provision.

Private Finance Initiative (Private – Public Partnership)

method of financing the use of capital assets in which part of the risk of investment is managed by the private sector.

Providers

a term used in the internal market. The provider must meet a defined level of service at a defined price. Usually refers to organisations, parts of organisations and individuals who provide care services on contract.

Psychological contract

a range of expectations of rights and privileges, duties and obligations which do not form part of a formal agreement but have an important influence on a person's behaviour.

Purchasing

a broad term which embraces the assessment of need, the appraisal of options to meet that need, including the sources of supply available from providers, and the decision about buying a service.

Quality

the totality of features and characteristics of a service that bear on its ability to satisfy a given need.

Quality assurance

all activities concerned with the attainment of quality.

Quality systems

formal systems to make certain that services consistently meet the standard required by services users and carers. These may be validated either within the service or by external auditors, or both.

Quality audit

the independent examination of quality to provide information.

Revenue budget

the estimate of a council's spending and income requirements. It also includes revenue financing of capital spending.

Revenue expenditure

spending on items which will benefit the organisation for less than one year: for example, a monthly salary.

Revenue support grant (RSG)

grant paid by the Government and designed to compensate for inequalities of need and resources among local authorities.

Service level agreement

a service agreement stating the nature and extent of services to be provided by one part of the organisation to another and how these are to be charged for.

Significant variations

substantial differences between actual and budgeted expenditure which require action in order to maintain overall performance.

Standing spending assessment (SSA)

the amount the Government considers appropriate for each local authority to spend to provide a standard level of service. It forms the basis of the Rate Support Grant distribution.

Strategy

the direction and scope of an organisation over the long term, which achieves advantage for the organisation, through the configuration of resources within a changing environment, and fufils stakeholder expectations.

Tender

a document which formalises the offer to supply goods or services to a defined level of quantity and quality for a price. A purchaser, (SSD) invites tenders and sets the specifications. Potential suppliers then define the price at which they are willing to supply. The purchaser is then in a position to choose which tender best meets their needs.

Transformational change

change which cannot be accommodated within the existing paradigm and organisational routines.

Service level agreement

written specification, usually for in-house services, between a central department and a service providing department or unit, specifying in detail the service to be provided, the volume to be purchased and quality of service.

Spreadsheet

the name given to a matrix format on a computer which provides a basis for numerical manipulation.

Strategy

the direction and scope of an organisation over the long term, which achieves advantage for the organisation through the configuration of resources within a changing environment, to meet the needs of, and fulfil, stakeholder expectations.

Unit cost

the full cost of supplying one item, arrived at by dividing total costs by the number of items.

Value for money

a buzz word in public sector financial management which implies getting the best return from resources. It incorporates:
- economy – minimising the use of resources
- efficiency – obtaining the maximum output from resources
- effectiveness – achieving the desired result.

A further 'e' often added is for 'equity'. This is concerned with the distribution of a service fairly to all those who need it.

Values

the principles which your organisation believes in and seeks to realise in everything it does. Values may be reflected in the department's mission, standards of work, relationships between individuals at work, relationships with suppliers, users and other stakeholders, personnel management and reward systems, training and development, equal opportunities, health and safety and environmental policies.

Virement

the power to move spending from one budget head to another budget head. Often used retrospectively to offset overspending on one budget head by underspending on another.

Variance

a difference between actual spending or income and what was planned in the budget.

Zero-based budgeting

a system of making a budget which is derived from actual need and other current commitments, without reference to budgets approved for previous periods and starting from scratch each year.

The following publications were used in compiling this glossary:

James, A. (1992) *Committed to Quality: Quality assurance in social services departments.* London: HSMO.

Jones, B. (1996) *Financial Management in the Public Sector.* London: McGraw-Hill.

Palmer, P. & Papaiacovou, C. (1990) *Beating the Budget.* Brighton: Pavilion.

Scragg, T. (1995) *Managing to Provide: A manual for managers of social care services.* Brighton: Pavilion.

TOPSS, England. (1999) *Modernising the Social Care Workforce: The first national training strategy for England.* London: Training Organisation for the Personal Social Services.

Also Available from Pavilion

A support manual for supervisees in health and social care

Jacky Knapman and Tony Morrison

This handbook is designed to help supervisees understand the process of clinical supervision and enable them to maximise the benefits of supervision sessions.

The text ensures that supervisees are as prepared and informed as their supervisors and stresses the importance of a partnership approach to supervision. The book presents ideas and information from a different perspective to most other titles on supervision, and is an ideal complement to Pavilion's best-selling Staff Supervision in Social Care.

Topics include: functions of supervision, benefits of supervision and choosing a supervisor.

Published by **Pavilion**

Format: **A4 manual (56pp).**

£14.95   Order Code 09P   ISBN: 1 900600 77 3

Pavilion